EXPLORE THE MUNROS

First published 2018
By Black & White Publishing Ltd
Nautical House, 104 Commercial Street,
Edinburgh, EH6 6NF

1 3 5 7 9 10 8 6 4 2   18 19 20 21

ISBN: 978 1 910230 58 9

Layout by Creative Link, Haddington
Printed and bound by Imago in Slovenia

THE Scots MAGAZINE

EXPLORE THE MUNROS

Your guide to 50 of Scotland's most iconic mountains

ROBERT WIGHT

BLACK & WHITE PUBLISHING

ADVICE TO READERS

Please note that every effort has been made by the author to ensure that the content of this book is as accurate and up-to-date as possible at the time of going to press. However, it is important to note that changes can occur over time to transport routes, rights of way, access, and in other ways, and it therefore remains the reader's sole responsibility to check and verify all information independently before setting out on any trip. If you do find that there have been changes or that any information in this book differs in any way from the reality on the ground, please email the details to mail@blackandwhitepublishing.com or write to the author, c/o Editor, The Scots Magazine, 1 Albert Square, Dundee DD1 1DD.

WARNING

Both hill walking and mountaineering can be hazardous activities which can carry the risk of personal injury or death. These activities require planning, knowledge and experience and should only be undertaken by those with suitable training and understanding of the risks involved. This book is intended as a guide only, and it remains the responsibility of all users to make themselves aware of the risks involved. In particular, weather conditions on the hills and mountains of Scotland can change very quickly at any time of year and this can have a material effect on any hill or mountain walk. Therefore, neither the publisher nor the author can accept any liability whatsoever for any damage of any kind, including damage to property, or personal injury or death, arising either directly or indirectly from the information in this book.

Anyone undertaking a hill or mountain walk, or any form of climbing excursion, should familiarise themselves with the number for Mountain Rescue. Dial 999 and ask for the police. The number for international rescue is 112 and will connect via any available network. The emergency operator can then direct your call.

IMAGE CREDITS

For my nephew Archie.
I hope this inspires you to explore the hills
when you're older.

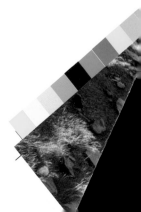

Loch Earn from Ben Vorlich

CONTENTS

CENTRAL HIGHLANDS

WESTERN HIGHLANDS

NORTHERN HIGHLANDS

THE CAIRNGORMS

Stob Dearg (Buachaille Etive Mor)

FOREWORD

by Cameron McNeish

ONE of Scotland's most marvellous features is the amazing diversity of landscape that is found here. Within 100 miles you can travel from the rugged Alpine-like grandeur of the Skye Cuillin to the massive dome-shaped Arctic hills of the Cairngorms, landscapes that couldn't be more different.

Or compare the ancient rocky formations of Torridon with the Angus Glens, or the rolling hills of the Borders, with the majestic peaks of Glen Coe or Glen Nevis.

Within many of these landscapes you'll find Munros, the 282 Scottish hills that top the 3000ft (914m) contour. The rich diversity of these hills is no less spectacular: surely one of the factors that has made Munro-bagging such a widespread and popular activity.

In this wonderful book Robert Wight, the *Scots Magazine* editor, has selected 50 of Scotland's Munros and described them in glorious detail in both words and images: here are 50 of the most impressive mountains in the land.

Just gazing at these images, imagining yourself climbing sun-kissed slopes or striving upwards into a winter wonderland, helps you understand the compulsion that has driven so many folk of all ages to take up the Munro challenge, a compulsion that is both addictive and hugely stimulating.

Climbing the Munros allows us to "connect" with these cherished landscapes in a way that develops our knowledge and appreciation of our indigenous wildlife, our history and folklore, and our Celtic/Norse heritage and culture.

The Munros may define the highest points in our magical country, but this book vividly portrays why these mountains contribute so much to what has been described as one of the most beautiful countries in the world.

Broadcaster and author Cameron McNeish is Scotland's leading authority on the outdoors. His latest book is There's Always The Hills *(2018).*

Ben Lomond and Loch Lomond

INTRODUCTION

THE Munros – Scotland's mountains of at least 3000ft (914m). There are 282 in all and climbing them is the ambition of many hillwalkers. Some rattle through the list in a few years. For others, it's the work of a lifetime.

This book is a photographic celebration of 50 selected Munros. Some are famous, iconic even – hugely popular hills such as Ben Nevis and Stob Dearg on Buachaille Etive Mor.

Others will be less well known, perhaps more remote and harder to get to. All are illustrated here by the most stunning imagery – wonderful photography that will make you want to head out there and discover the hills for real.

Indeed, that's the aim of this book – to inspire readers to get outside and explore.

As well as incredible photographs, each of the 50 chapters comes with short descriptive passages outlining interesting facts and features about the hills. In addition, rather than set out prescriptive, exhaustively detailed "A to B" routes, I give a rough overview of a route I recommend – the idea is to spark your imagination. Get the maps and guidebooks out, pore over them and design your own adventures.

Information panels for recommended routes give details including heights, walk lengths and amount of ascent. Times should be treated as a rough guide for a reasonably fit walker making minimal, brief stops. Times can vary considerably depending on fitness and conditions – in winter snows, you'll need to add on a couple of extra hours at least.

Often, there's more than one approach to a hill, and more than one way to climb a hill. With this is mind, distances to nearest towns are measured directly and from the summit – the idea is to give an indication of the proximity of the nearest suitable base.

I finished my own Munro round in June 2017. I've climbed quite a lot of them twice, and some of them many more times – which is why I decided to start "ticking" the list in the first place. I'd become a lazy hillwalker, returning to the same areas time and again – Lochaber and Glencoe, the Arrochar Alps, the Cairngorms. Working my way through the Munros would, I figured, force me to broaden my hillwalking horizons and take me to new places.

For me, that's the great pleasure of "bagging" Munros – you experience places you'd never otherwise see. To complete the Munros – or "compleat", tradition dictates the archaic spelling is used – usually requires camping trips and bothy stays in the most remote, wild landscapes; areas most people never venture.

It's a huge privilege to visit such places, among the most beautiful and untouched in Scotland. The memories made will be cherished for life.

So what are you waiting for? Happy Exploring!

EXPLORING THE MUNROS

The Mamores from Am Bodach

Ben Nevis and the Allt a' Mhuilinn Trail

WHAT IS A MUNRO?

MUNROS are named after Sir Hugh Munro (1856–1919), a founding member of the Scottish Mountaineering Club (SMC).

In 1891, he published his "Tables", a list of Scottish mountains thought to be 3000ft (914m) or higher. Before this, no one had any real idea of how many such mountains Scotland had, and it was the subject of much debate among early climbers.

Sir Hugh was charged by the editor of the SMC's journal with laying the matter to rest. Using the Ordnance Survey's six-inches-to-the-mile maps – notoriously short on detail – and his own considerable experience, he calculated that there were 283 mountains above 3000ft. They were soon to become known as "Munros".

In addition, Sir Hugh listed a further 255 "Tops" – these are summits also higher than 3000ft but not distinct enough to be regarded as "separate" mountains.

It wasn't long after the list was published that hillwalkers' thoughts turned to climbing them all. The first "Munroist" was the Reverend A. E. Robertson, in 1901. He "compleated" on Meall Dearg in Glencoe, famously kissing first the cairn and then his wife.

Subsequent research has cast doubt on whether Robertson actually compleated in 1901 – his diaries mention turning back on Ben Wyvis in heavy rain, suggesting, perhaps, that he didn't reach the summit.

Sir Hugh didn't manage to compleat his own list, dying in 1919 with three hills unclimbed.

Over the years there have been several revisions. Indeed, Sir Hugh was working on such a revision when he died. As surveying techniques improved and equipment became more accurate, hills were added and removed from the list. As of 2018, there are 282 Munros and a further 227 Tops.

The Tables continue to be maintained by the SMC. Munroists can contact the SMC's Clerk of the List – in writing only – to register their achievement. They're assigned a compleation number and receive a certificate. More than 6000 compleations had been registered in 2018. For more information visit www.smc.org.uk.

NAVIGATION & SAFETY

EVERY hillwalker should carry a map and compass, and know how to use them properly. This is a real skill – and an essential one to practise for your own safety and wellbeing out on the hills.

Digital mapping and hand-held GPS devices are fantastic tools – but they should be carried in addition to a compass and paper map, not in place of them. If you do carry them, take extra batteries.

Walk with more experienced friends – or better yet join a hillwalking club. Most are more than happy to share their knowledge. There are also many outdoor education providers who run day courses, on which you'll learn a lot.

The following pointers are essential to ensure your safety on the hills.

- In a group, everyone should carry their own map and compass, in case of separation. If you're out on your own, you should carry a second map and compass. It might sound like overkill, but maps do blow away, and compasses are easily broken. Better to be safe.

- I tend to carry a map in a waterproof bag in my pack, and a photocopy of the section that includes my route in a see-through plastic wallet. This means I can fold the photocopy and carry it in a pocket. It makes it much easier to refer to.

- I usually use Ordnance Survey 1:50,000 Landranger maps. Most routes fit nicely on a couple of panels when it's folded down. The 1:25,000 Explorer maps give more detail but I find them cumbersome. Routes tend to cover several panels, meaning you often have to unfold and refold it during the walk – not always the easiest in wet and windy weather. Sometimes this folding and unfolding is needed to find the grid numbers as well.

- The others I use are 1:25,000 Harvey Superwalker maps – they cover many of Scotland's most popular mountain areas and are designed with walkers in mind. They're printed on waterproof paper and some include "blow-ups" of certain areas on the reverse – for example a 1:12,500 map of the Cuillin ridge.

- Always leave a note of your route and expected time of return with a friend or relative, or even with your accommodation provider if staying at a hotel or hostel. Route cards, on which all relevant information can be written, are a great idea and can be left on your car's dashboard. This can be a lifesaver if you get into unexpected difficulties.

AVALANCHES ❄

ENTIRE books have been written about the dangers of avalanches and assessing their risk. Indeed, the "go to" publication is *A Chance in a Million?*, by Bob Barton and Blyth Wright.

The basics can be learned on Winter Skills courses run by the likes of the National Outdoor Training Centre at Glenmore Lodge. They also run specialised Avalanche Awareness courses. Fatal avalanche accidents occur most winters in Scotland and any slope between 22 and 60 degrees should be treated with caution – particularly after heavy snows or periods of thaw.

Visit the Scottish Avalanche Information Service website (www.sais.gov.uk) and

Northern Corries to Cairn Lochan

learn how to use their detailed reports and hazard summaries.

Walkers should also study forecasts in the days leading up to hill trips, studying temperatures, snowfall amounts and wind direction to work out on which slopes snow has been deposited. If in any doubt about a snow slope – don't risk it.

FORECASTS

THE Mountain Weather Information Service (MWIS) is the most useful forecasting resource for hillwalkers.

Their website – www.mwis.org.uk – splits Scotland into five mountain areas: the North-west Highlands, West Highlands, Cairngorms National Park and Monadhliath, South-eastern Highlands and Southern Uplands.

Detailed forecasts for the following three days are posted by 4.30p.m. every day, earlier in winter.

The Met Office website gives a six-day forecast, allowing you to enter individual hill names in the location search bar. See www.metoffice.gov.uk.

They also have a dedicated mountain weather section, splitting Scotland into four areas – North-west Highlands, North Grampian, South Grampian and South-east Highlands, and South-west Highlands.

ACCESS

SCOTLAND'S outdoor access laws are among the most progressive in the world.

The Land Reform Act (2003) sets out the statutory "right to roam", granting largely unfettered access to most land and inland waterways. With some restrictions, it includes wild camping.

With that right comes responsibilities, as laid out in the Scottish Outdoor Access Code, which is based on three key principles:

- **Respect the interests of other people.**
  Acting with courtesy, consideration and awareness is very important. If you are exercising access rights, make sure that you respect the privacy, safety and livelihoods of those living or working in the outdoors, and the needs of other people enjoying the outdoors. If you are a land manager, respect people's use of the outdoors and their need for a safe and enjoyable visit.

- **Care for the environment.**
  If you are exercising access rights, look after the places you visit and enjoy, and leave the land as you find it. If you are a land manager, help maintain the natural and cultural features that make the outdoors attractive to visit and enjoy.

- **Take responsibility for your own actions.**
  If you are exercising access rights, remember that the outdoors cannot be made risk-free and act with care at all times for your own safety and that of others. If you are a land manager, act with care at all times for people's safety.

Further information can be found on the Scottish Outdoor Access Code website at www.outdooraccess-scotland.scot.

DEER STALKING

THE stag stalking season runs from July 1 to October 20. Many estates request that walkers avoid specific areas at certain times during that period – usually corries. Ridges are normally fine.

There's no legal obligation to comply, but doing so helps build good relations with landowners. Most estates suggest alternative routes and there are plenty of areas where there's no stalking at all. Stalking doesn't take place on Sundays.

The "Heading For The Scottish Hills" section on the Scottish Outdoor Access Code website provides excellent information on where and when stalking takes place.

EQUIPMENT & CLOTHING

ANYONE who spends any time in the Scottish hills is going to get cold and wet, even in summer. Waterproofs should always be carried. Over-trousers with full-length side zips are most convenient. Good quality, breathable and warm outer-shell jackets can be expensive, but full waterproof cover makes life much more comfortable and is money well spent.

Other clothing and equipment to consider.

Boots – if you get one pair of boots, I'd recommend three-season leather boots. They can be used most of the year and in my experience are easier to clean, keep waterproof and last longer than fabric boots. The downside is they tend to be heavier.

In good weather and on easier ground, trail shoes are a good lightweight option. Whatever your choice, your footwear should have excellent, hard-wearing, grippy soles made from a material such as Vibram.

Base layers – should be made of a wicking material that carries moisture and perspiration away from the body. Merino wool is excellent – it's warm, quick drying and comfortable. It also tends not to smell. . . Avoid cotton – once wet it stays wet and leaches the heat from your body.

Trousers – full-length to protect against ticks and jaggy plants. Avoid denims for the same reasons as cotton base layers.

Tops – a light fleece over a base layer is all most will need in summer. Always pack a mid-weight fleece as well in case it gets chilly.

Hat and gloves – even in summer these are a must. Snow and sleet can be encountered on summits in June, and wind-chill can make it feel very cold at any time.

Snood – a stretchy tube of material that's hugely versatile. Can be used as a neck warmer, headband, hat or balaclava.

Gaiters – a must in winter as they prevent snow from getting up trouser legs. In summer, they help protect against ticks and keep legs and feet drier. They also stop stones, twigs and other debris from getting in your boots.

Pack – a 25-litre pack is fine for day walks in summer. In winter, when extra kit is required, 35 litres is more appropriate. Most packs these days have padded hip belts, which help distribute weight and keep the pack steady on your body.

Walking poles – these have become increasingly popular in recent years. Two poles lessen the stress on knees by distributing weight. They're great when carrying heavy loads. Telescopic poles are most convenient as they're easy to stow. I always carry one pole – it's useful for river-crossings, aiding balance on difficult terrain and can be used as a crutch in the event of twisting an ankle.

WINTER KIT

IN winter, hillwalking in Scotland becomes mountaineering and you will need specialist kit. Just as important as the extra gear, are the knowledge and skills to use it. Anyone venturing out in winter should consider attending one of the excellent Winter Skills Courses, such as those on offer at Glenmore Lodge, home of the Scottish National Outdoor Training Centre.

In addition to all your summer kit, you'll need stiff-soled boots rated for crampon use, as well as the crampons. Boots are rated B1, B2 and B3. In the most basic terms, the higher the number, the stiffer the sole. Similarly, crampons are rated C1, C2 and C3. Boots should never be combined with higher-rated crampons (although the reverse doesn't apply).

The type of boot and crampon you need will depend on what you plan to do in the hills in winter. Climbers will use B3 boots and C3 crampons. Most walkers will be fine with B1 and C1s.

Many novice walkers don't ever imagine themselves as climbers, until they experience the thrill of the mountains in winter. As these items are expensive and will be used for many years, a good option is B2 boots and C2 crampons – they're comfortable enough for a day's walking but stiff enough to tackle simple winter gullies at Grade 1 or 2. Before spending several hundred pounds, research the options and seek out advice from more experienced friends and experts from respected outdoor retailers.

Walker's ice axe – this is essential as it can be used to self-arrest in the event of a trip or slip on icy slopes, as well as cutting steps in steep snow and ice. Again, research the options, seek advice and make sure you know how to use it.

Goggles – these will protect the eyes and face, which can make all the difference when the wind's blowing a hoolie.

Extra clothing – the hills are cold in winter. Wrap up – layering is the key as they trap air that is warmed by your body. A spare hat and at least one spare pair of gloves should be carried. Gloves get wet and cold quickly, plus the wind can carry them off. A belay – or duvet – jacket is great for extended stops. Buy synthetic rather than down as they retain heat even when wet. Down doesn't. A balaclava in addition to a hat is also a good idea.

EMERGENCY EQUIPMENT

THESE are rucksack essentials – hopefully you'll never need them, but they should always be carried.

First-Aid Kit – outdoor-gear shops sell ready-packed first-aid kits with everything you need. As a minimum, you should pack plasters of varying sizes, dressings, medical/

antiseptic wipes, micro-pore tape and a tick remover, all in a waterproof container.

Whistle – vital for signalling distress. The internationally recognised signal is six blasts, a minute's gap, then another six blasts. Rescuers will respond with three whistle blasts, but keep repeating the signal until you're certain they can actually see you.

Torch – In winter especially, benightment is a real risk. A navigational error, deep snow slowing progress – it doesn't take much to go wrong and use up the light on short days. A headtorch is best as it keeps your hands free.

A torch can also be used to signal distress – use it just like a whistle, flashing the light instead. If a rescue helicopter is summoned, don't shine the light at it – it could dazzle the pilot. I carry a headtorch – and replacement batteries – year-round.

Survival bag – this is a large, heavy-duty plastic bag you can climb into in the event of an emergency. It'll keep you warm but – being plastic – condensation will build up and you'll get pretty damp. It could, however, make all the difference if push comes to shove.

Emergency rations – some spare food – ideally high-calorie and easy to eat, like a flapjack or chocolate bars. I keep a couple of muesli bars alongside my first-aid kit.

MIDGES, CLEGS & TICKS

MIDGES are the curse of the Scottish summer. The tiny, flying bloodsuckers are active from around the beginning of June until into September.

The insects thrive in mild, damp, heavily vegetated or wooded environments and where standing water – such as lochs or pools – is present. They're usually most active in the morning and at dusk, once the heat of the sun is gone.

It's hard to convey to someone who has never experienced it just how unpleasant a full-on midge attack is. Swarms, thousands strong, can descend in seconds. Any exposed flesh feels like it's crawling. Victims – usually getting changed at the car, or putting on boots – are driven to distraction. In Glen Etive, I've experienced clouds of midges so thick I was actually choking on them.

Reactions to bites vary – some experience a small red dot that disappears in a day. Others blow up in lumpy, itchy swellings.

Various insecticide sprays are available. Some swear by the Avon Skin So Soft spray – apparently midges hate it and you'll find it for sale in shops across the Highlands. Head nets are another option. But my best advice is to keep moving – the slightest breeze defeats the pests.

CLEGS – or horseflies – are the opposite of midges, in the sense that they're quite big and yet you usually don't feel them on your skin . . . at least not at first. They have very sharp mouthparts which they use to lacerate the skin before lapping the flowing blood. Their saliva contains an anticoagulant, so the blood can keep flowing long after you've swatted the pest. The bite causes a raised, painful red welt. Like midges, they're active in the summer months.

TICKS are the big danger in Scotland's hills as they can carry disease, most notably Lyme disease – a horribly debilitating illness if left untreated.

Ticks are arachnids. As parasites, they feed on the blood of other creatures. They're very small and hard to spot – and their bite is painless. Usually you don't see them until they've attached themselves by burrowing their heads into your skin. They can remain there for days, slowly swelling as they gorge on your blood.

The two types most likely to affect hillwalkers are sheep and deer ticks – be extra vigilant in areas with high numbers of these animals, but they can be found anywhere where there is vegetation like grass or bracken. They climb to the edge of plants where they wait for passing animals or people to brush past. They then hitch a ride and find somewhere suitable to bite – usually somewhere warm and dark like armpits, groins, under waistbands or sock tops.

If you find a tick, it's important to remove the whole creature – simply plucking it off can leave the head buried in your skin. A specialised tick remover or hook costs pennies and is a worthwhile addition to a first-aid kit.

I always wear long trousers on the hills – even on the hottest days. Tuck trouser legs in socks, or better yet wear gaiters. If I'm going somewhere where I know I'll be walking in long grass or bracken, I'll spray insecticide on my boots and gaiters.

Once you get home, give yourself a thorough check. Lyme disease, if caught early, can be treated with antibiotics. Symptoms can be flu-like and include fatigue and muscle and joint pain. Sometimes a characteristic "bullseye" rash appears. If in any doubt, consult your doctor – and remember to tell them you've been hillwalking.

Rock pool, near
the Ring of Steall

BOTHIES

BOTHIES are unlocked shelters in mountainous and remote areas, open for anyone to use. There are scores across Scotland. The Mountain Bothy Association (MBA) maintain around one hundred of them, and most are owned by the estates on which they lie. Others are looked after by the estates themselves. They're usually old estate cottages, or shepherd's or stalker's huts. All are open for use thanks to the generosity of the estates that own them.

Follow these simple rules when staying in a bothy – they really do depend on a community-minded spirit.

- Some have stoves or open fireplaces, but you will need to carry your fuel in.

- Any rubbish should be carried out.

- Human waste should be buried downstream and well away from any water source and the bothy itself.

- Be sure to leave the bothy in at least as clean a condition as you found it.

As hillwalking has grown in popularity so too have bothies – and they can become very busy. They shouldn't be relied upon for accommodation and carrying a tent is advisable.

Users should follow the "bothy code", which can be viewed on the MBA website, www.mountainbothies.org.uk.

Luib Chonnal bothy, upper Glen Roy

Bynack More and Bynack Beg

Southern Highlands from Beinn Narnain

SOUTHERN
HIGHLANDS

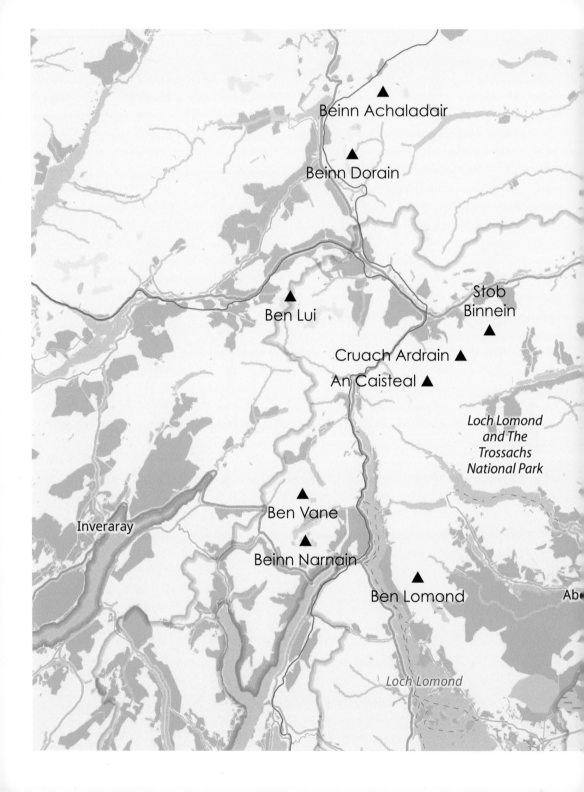

Did You Know?

A Royal Navy torpedo range was situated on Loch Long near the start of this walk. It operated from 1912 to 1986. It burned down in 2007 but the site remains popular with divers.

The Cobbler from Beinn Narnain

1

Beinn Narnain

PART of the compact cluster of Munros and Corbetts known as "the Arrochar Alps", Beinn Narnain is a hugely popular hill.

It's one of the lower Munros, scraping that status by just 12m (39ft), making it 259th in the Munro tables – but don't be fooled into thinking it's a "lesser" hill. Like its neighbours, Beinn Narnain is a very steep, rugged little mountain. And, if following the route recommended here, the climb starts from barely above sea level, so you haul yourself up every metre.

The Arrochar Alps hold a special place in Scottish mountaineering history – the area was central to the development of climbing in the country in the 19th century. Partly, that's due to the area's proximity to Scotland's largest city, Glasgow, and the ease of access afforded by the West Highland Railway Line, with its station in Arrochar.

Mostly it's due to the wonderful hills themselves, in particular the Corbett Ben Arthur, better known as "the Cobbler". Its three summit peaks – the outer two appearing as gnarled, curving horns – provide one of the most distinctive mountain outlines in Scotland and are visible from many miles away. They remain a lure for climbers and it's a great venue for rock climbing. The route suggested here

Pronunciation: *Ben Nar-nain*
Meaning: notched hill
Height: 926m (3038ft); Rank: 259
OS Landranger Map 56
Summit grid ref: NN271066 (trig point)

gives wonderful views of the Cobbler on approach.

Beinn Narnain can be linked with several of its neighbours and is commonly climbed with Beinn Ime, or indeed the Cobbler. Those seeking more of a challenge can add in the Munro Ben Vane for a three-Munro circuit, starting from Inveruglas on Loch Lomond.

As a single hill, its proximity to the A83 roadside means there's little in the way of a walk in, which makes it a fantastic choice for a short winter day.

Whatever your route, pick your day and you'll be rewarded with breathtaking views down the length of Loch Long to the Kyles of Bute beyond.

Beinn Ime from Beinn Narnain

Ben Lomond from Beinn Narnain

NEAREST TOWN: Arrochar is about 4km (2.5 miles) south-east. Heart of the Arrochar Alps, it's a popular base for mountaineers, with a variety of accommodation from bunkhouses, camping and a caravan park to B&Bs and hotels. There are small shops, a petrol station and places to eat and drink.

RECOMMENDED ROUTE
Start grid ref: NN294048
Distance: 9km (5.6 miles)
Ascent: 950m (3117ft)
Time: 4.5hrs

THE ROUTE

This walk starts at the Forestry Commission car park – for use of which you need to pay – just around the head of Loch Long on the north shore near Succoth. It's also the main car park for the trade route up the Cobbler and Beinn Ime and is normally very busy. Best to get there early.

Cross the road to join a path that takes you steeply up through some woodland. Soon you're on open hillside, where a line of concrete blocks can be followed. They're the bases of an old rail track from the time of the construction of the nearby dam and hydro-electric scheme at Loch Sloy.

Continue north-west. The nature of the hill changes and it begins to feel much rockier and mountainous. A couple of very easy scrambling sections give some fun and soon dramatic views of the Cobbler open up.

The route goes over Cruach nam Miseag and soon you're confronted by the famous Spearhead – a towering buttress of rock. It's easily tackled by a path to the right, up a rocky gully to the plateau. From here, the trig point lies a couple of hundred metres east.

For the return, head north-west to the Bealach a' Mhaim. From here, both Beinn Ime and the Cobbler are realistic targets. If you can't be tempted, follow the excellent path past the Narnain Boulders south-east about 5km (3.1 miles) back to the car park.

Glen Croe from the Rest And Be Thankfu

REST AND BE THANKFUL

Nearby lies one of Scotland's most famous mountain passes – the romantically named "Rest And Be Thankful".

The Rest, as it's often referred to, is the high point of the A83 trunk road and separates Glen Croe from Glen Kinglass. It's a popular viewpoint and picnic spot. Along the floor of the valley twists the "old road" following the route of the original military road constructed in the 1750s by General Wade's troops. It was they who gave the pass its colourful name.

The modern road runs along the steep hillside, a few tens of metres above the old route. It's a notorious area for landslides, particularly after heavy autumn and winter rains, and they've caused the road to be temporarily closed many times over the years. Substantial engineering works have attempted to reduce the impact of the landslides – but the narrow single track of the old route is kept in good repair, just in case!

Did You Know?

The massive lumps of rock known as the Narnain Boulders were used as a traditional meeting place and overnight shelter for generations of climbers from Glasgow. Today, they're a popular lunch spot for walkers.

Narnain Boulders

Loch Long from Beinn Narnain

Ben Vane

Beinn Narnain from Ben Vane

2

Ben Vane

THIS lovely wee hill – another of the immensely popular Arrochar Alps group – is Scotland's smallest Munro, edging into the list by less than a metre.

But what Ben Vane lacks in height, it makes up for in character. Like the Jack Russell that squares up to Alsatians, this is a hill that thinks it's a mountain.

Its name is an anglicisation of the Gaelic for "middle hill", and it's neatly encircled by the Munros Ben Vorlich, Beinn Narnain and Beinn Ime.

Like the other hills in this group, Ben Vane's proximity to Glasgow – and ease of access – means it attracts a lot of walkers. Because of this, the normal route – which is also the route suggested here – is very eroded, the path at times a thigh-deep trench slinking up the hillside, and the approach a boggy mess.

At the time of writing, the British Mountaineering Council – working with Mountaineering Scotland and the Outdoor Access Trust for Scotland, among others – is campaigning to raise funds to restore the route.

Ben Vane, I think, is the perfect hill for a crisp, snowy, winter's day out – it's a short, sharp climb and there's no big walk in as it's pretty close to the road. I wouldn't recommend it as a first-ever

> Pronunciation: *Ben Vay-ann*
> Meaning: middle hill
> Height: 915m (3002ft); Rank: 282
> OS Landranger Map 56
> Summit grid ref: NN277098 (cairn)

winter hill as there are a couple of rocky steps toward the summit. They're perfectly straightforward, but might be a bit of a challenge for the novice – particularly in descent if visibility is poor. Good route-finding is essential. For those with a bit of experience, however, the brief scrambling sections provide a welcome bit of added interest.

A winter freeze means the initial bog-fest is a much more pleasant prospect. Frozen terrain and snow cover also mean you'll contribute little to the erosion scarring the land.

The conical hill stands alone and, although not the tallest, the summit feels nice and airy. Views of the surrounding Arrochar Alps are wonderful and to the north lies massive Ben Lui.

What draws the eye, though, is the vast expanse of Loch Lomond, studded with its many islands and stretching far to the south.

Ben Vorlich from Ben Vane

NEAREST TOWN: Arrochar is only 6.5km (4 miles) away but Balloch, 31km (19.3 miles) south, is also a convenient centre with more amenities, including plenty of bars, restaurants and accommodation. It's also home to Loch Lomond SEA LIFE Aquarium – a great option when the weather's too miserable for the hills!

RECOMMENDED ROUTE
Start grid ref: NN322098
Distance: 11.2km (7 miles)
Ascent: 950m (3117ft)
Time: 4.5hrs

THE ROUTE

Ben Vane might be our smallest Munro but it's very rocky and steep. Its solitary position also means linking it with any of the other Arrochar Alps makes for big days, perhaps not in terms of distance, but certainly in ascent.

The easiest option is to tackle it on its own from Inveruglas, where there's a visitor centre and a car park (£4 charge for the day at time of printing).

Head south along the A82 from the car park past the hydro-electric power station for about 1km (0.6 miles), then head right up a tarmac road under the railway. This section of the walk isn't terribly attractive thanks to power lines and other infrastructure associated with the Loch Sloy dam, but soon the rocky pyramid of Ben Vane lures you on.

After 2km (1.2 miles) leave the tarmac road for a rougher track heading left. It crosses a bridge. Shortly after this you'll reach a smaller bridge – here a clear path heads to the right and the boggy approach to Ben Vane.

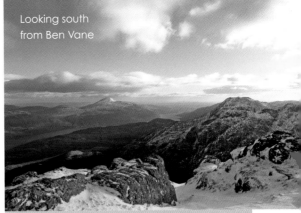

Looking south
from Ben Vane

The route from here follows the hill's south-east ridge – a steep wee climb. Rocky outcrops and crags give some options for scramblers but sticking to the zig-zagging path avoids any serious difficulties. The path takes you over a few false summits before the top is reached.

Ascending Ben Vane

LOCH SLOY

The massive pipes running down the hillside at Inveruglas, the turbine house, huge pylons, power station and dammed loch you pass on approach to Ben Vane are all part of the Loch Sloy Hydro-Electric Scheme.

Construction began in 1945 and finished in 1949. The initial workforce included many German prisoners of war.

The scheme, which includes a 3km (1.9 mile) tunnel through Ben Vorlich, was officially opened in 1950 by Queen Elizabeth, later the Queen Mother.

The dam, which runs between the foot of Ben Vane and Ben Vorlich, doubled the size of the original loch and raised its level by almost 50m (164ft).

The scheme remains the largest conventional hydro-electric plant in the UK, and its four turbines can provide enough power for 50,000 homes.

Loch Sloy was chosen for the scheme for a simple reason – with an annual rainfall of over 3000mm (118in), it's one of the wettest parts of Scotland.

Ben Lomond and Loch Lomond

Ptarmigan Ridge

Did You Know?

Loch Lomond is 39km (24.2 miles) long and has the largest surface area of any fresh water body in the UK. Among its many islands is Inchmurrin – the largest freshwater island in the UK.

3
Ben Lomond

S COTLAND'S most southerly Munro lies on the rugged and beautiful eastern shore of Loch Lomond, just 59.5km (37 miles) from Glasgow, the country's largest city.

It's a solitary hill that dominates its surroundings and is visible from many miles away, indeed from far south of Glasgow where it appears as a broad, hulking mass.

From the north and west, the sharp profile of the mountain's Ptarmigan Ridge is prominent and the summit appears as a pyramid.

My own favourite view is from the east, from the shores of Loch Ard, near Aberfoyle. It's from here that I think Ben Lomond looks like a proper mountain, towering over the loch and land, its graceful summit cone seeming almost volcanic.

An excellent path – including sections of stone steps – leads from Rowardennan, making an ascent by this route straightforward. This, and its location on Glasgow's doorstep, makes Ben Lomond one of Scotland's busiest Munros, with more than 30,000 walking to the top each year.

Despite its popularity and ease of access, it's important to remember this is still a Munro and should be treated with respect – weather conditions at height

Pronunciation: *Ben Low-mond*
Meaning: beacon hill
Height: 974m (3196ft); Rank: 184
OS Landranger Map 56
Summit grid ref: NN367028 (trig point)

can quickly deteriorate, and appropriate clothing and equipment should be carried. In winter, this means an ice axe and crampons, as well as the knowledge and experience to use them.

Like many Glaswegians, Ben Lomond was my first Munro as a teenager. I'm not sure I even knew what Munros were at the time – this was just a mountain I'd seen on the horizon since I was a child and I was determined I'd climb it one day.

It was late spring, and I remember the views from the summit left me speechless – to the south, spread before me like a map, lay Loch Lomond, its crystal waters reflecting the pale blue of the early-morning sky and its many, forested islands looking as green as emeralds.

Beyond was the vast sprawl of Glasgow and its high-rise flats – even it looked impressive to me.

But it was the north that really excited me – here were myriad other peaks, row upon row of distant mountains, the furthest still wearing crowns of snow and every one

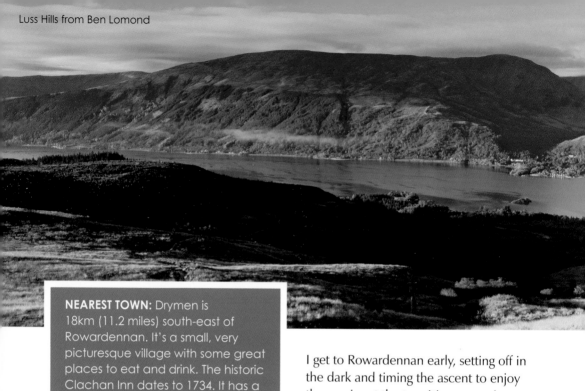

Luss Hills from Ben Lomond

NEAREST TOWN: Drymen is 18km (11.2 miles) south-east of Rowardennan. It's a small, very picturesque village with some great places to eat and drink. The historic Clachan Inn dates to 1734. It has a small supermarket, a couple of inns/hotels and plenty of B&B options.

RECOMMENDED ROUTE
Start grid ref: NS359986
Distance: 11km (6.8 miles)
Ascent: 1000m (3281ft)
Time: 5hrs

completely unknown to me. I knew I'd explore them all.

I've climbed Ben Lomond many times since – I've no idea how many – and the view remains one of my favourites of any hill. Certainly it's one of the best vistas in the Southern Highlands.

Other than Ben Nevis, it's the busiest summit I've ever experienced – you can share it with dozens of others. Sometimes,

I get to Rowardennan early, setting off in the dark and timing the ascent to enjoy the sunrise at the top. It's an amazing experience, and if I'm lucky I get the top to myself. What a privilege.

THE ROUTE

Start at Rowardennan, where there's a car park run by the Forestry Commission (£3 charge for the day).

The easiest ascent is up and down the excellent "tourist path" and will take roughly four hours for a reasonably fit walker.

The route I recommend, however, takes you up the Ptarmigan Ridge and is much more interesting, while avoiding the worst of the crowds – although it's now also pretty busy, particularly in summer.

Head north from the car park for about 1km (0.6 miles). Just beyond a small clutch

36

Did You Know?

Ben Lomond sits almost directly on the Highland Boundary Fault Line, a major geological feature that separates the Highlands from the Lowlands and which runs diagonally from Arran in the west to Stonehaven in the east.

A UNIQUE STEAM SHIP

A few kilometres north-east of Ben Lomond lies Loch Katrine, the scenic Trossachs' loch that for almost 160 years has supplied much of Glasgow's water supply, thanks to an impressive feat of Victorian engineering.

A network of aqueducts and tunnels carries water, under force of gravity, 41.5km (26 miles) from the loch to reservoirs north of the city. The tunnels – bored through solid rock – were dug by hand in the days before pneumatic tools were available.

The loch is also home to the SS *Sir Walter Scott* – the only surviving screw-driven steamer in regular passenger service in Scotland.

The historic ship was built at Dumbarton in 1899 by William Denny and Brothers. It was then disassembled, transported by barge to Inversnaid on Loch Lomond, just north of the Ben, and then by horse and cart to Stronachlachar on Loch Katrine. Workers from Denny's then reassembled the ship, which continues to sail using its original triple-expansion steam engine.

of buildings at Ardess, a path heads to the right and soon rises steeply uphill – follow this on to the Ptarmigan Ridge. The path is well-worn and muddy at times and eventually reaches the minor peak of Ptarmigan itself.

From here head north-east to the bealach and then on to Lomond's north-west ridge. The views south to the loch are quite simply stunning – this is a route to save for a clear day.

Minor scrambling takes you directly to the summit and trig point.

Descending via the tourist path makes for a pleasing circuit. Head south-east off the summit cone – on clear days you'll get the chance to appreciate the mountain's most impressive feature, its wide north-east corrie. There are steep cliffs here, plunging almost 100m (330ft), which the path skirts quite close to – take care in bad weather.

A flatter area of ground is reached and the obvious path turns south, then south-west after a few kilometres and back to Rowardennan.

Ben Lomond

Ben Vorlich and Stuc a' Chroin

Did You Know?

Despite being landlocked, Loch Earn has its own mini tidal system, known as a "seiche". It's caused by the strength of the prevailing wind.

Ben Our from Ben Vorlich

4

Ben Vorlich

SITTING apart from any other Munros, Ben Vorlich and its neighbour Stuc a' Chroin completely dominate this part of the Southern Highlands.

Ben Vorlich – which shares its name with another Munro found in the Arrochar Alps – looks quite different depending on one's viewpoint. But in every case it's an incredibly distinctive and easily recognised mountain.

The hill can be seen for many miles in all directions, and its situation on the northern edge of the heavily populated Central Belt means it's very popular.

From the south, Ben Vorlich appears like a giant Viking hogback tomb. It's well seen for a considerable distance on approach to Stirling, providing a magnificent mountain backdrop to the picturesque city's fairy-tale castle and imposing monument to Sir William Wallace.

From other directions, the mountain is an elegant, symmetrical pyramid of a peak.

There are several possible routes up the hill. The most direct – which I recommend here and that can easily be extended to take in Stuc a' Chroin – is from Ardvorlich, on the southern shores of beautiful Loch Earn.

Climbing the peak as a there-and-back

Pronunciation: *Ben Vor-lich*
Meaning: hill of the bay
Height: 985m (3232ft); Rank: 165
OS Landranger Maps 51 & 57
Summit grid ref: NN629189 (trig point)

from Ardvorlich is a relatively quick day out – making it a super choice for a short winter day. The road to the start, however, is a single track that twists along the lochside, and passing places are few and far between. Care must be taken driving it in wintry weather.

Ben Vorlich sits just north of the Highland Boundary Fault Line, a fact that's abundantly clear from the summit. To the south, views of rolling hills and flat lands extend to the Border hills, while to the north, the great rumpled mountains of the rugged Highlands fill the horizon.

There are a couple of Corbetts in the area – Beinn Each, to the south-west of Stuc a' Chroin, and Meall na Fearna, to the east of Ben Vorlich. A traverse of all four hills is a marvellous day out – although up to about 30km (18.5 miles), with almost 2000m (6562ft) of ascent. Start in Glen Ample to take in Beinn Each first. The route takes you to Ardvorlich so it's necessary to either leave a car here or arrange transport.

Beinn Domhnuill from Ben Vorlich

THE ROUTE

A rough layby on the south side of the narrow single-track access road, just east of Ardvorlich House, provides parking for several vehicles.

The route initially heads south on the right-of-way path that eventually leads to Callander. Follow the excellent track for about 1.5km (1 mile) to a junction, at which you take the right fork.

After a short distance, the path crosses the Allt a' Choire Bhuidhe and climbs a grassy ridge, heading south all the time.

The Munro is a very popular hill and the path, eroded in places, is very clear all the way up the north ridge. The final section is rather steep and takes you quickly to the trig point. A cairn sits 100m (330ft) east, slightly lower that the trig point. With the expanse of the Lowlands laid out to the south and, other than Stuc a' Chroin, no nearby Munros, the summit feels wonderfully airy.

Most Munro-baggers will want to continue to Stuc a' Chroin. In fine weather the way ahead is obvious, and there's also a line of old fence posts that lead south-west down steep, grassy ground to the Bealach an Dubh Choirein.

A path leads to a scree field littered with large rocks. Above this sits the enormous buttress, up which you scramble to reach the Munro's north top. The scramble can look intimidating, but up close the rock

Loch Earn at dawn

is well-worn by thousands of feet and hands, and the route is quite obvious. It is, however, very loose in sections and not something for novice scramblers to attempt.

It can be avoided by descending north for a short distance at the bealach to pick up an increasingly steep path to the north-west ridge. The actual summit is roughly 0.5km (0.3 miles) south.

On the return, the buttress is avoided by a path that initially follows the north-west ridge, gradually curving east to below the bealach. From here it's possible to contour round the west flank of Ben Vorlich and eventually pick up the track back to Ardvorlich.

ARDVORLICH HOUSE

At its start, the route up Ben Vorlich described here passes through the grounds of Ardvorlich House.

It was built in 1790 by Robert Ferguson on the site of an earlier castle, some of the walls of which were incorporated into the new structure.

For 400 years it's been the seat of the Stewarts of Ardvorlich. The current owner is the 15th laird, Alexander Stewart.

The house was visited by novelist Sir Walter Scott and is said to be the inspiration for the castle Darnlinvarach in his 1819 novel *A Legend of Montrose*. The story is set during the 1640s, while the Civil War raged in England. In Scotland, the Earl of Montrose led a campaign against the Covenanters, who had sided with the English Parliament.

Legends associated with Ardvorlich provided Scott with inspiration for his plot, including the dark tale of how MacGregors killed John Drummond and cruelly presented his head to his sister, Lady Margaret of Ardvorlich.

Stuc a' Chroin from Ben Vorlich

Did You Know?

The Falls of Falloch, a beautiful waterfall and popular picnic spot, lie just off the A82, a few kilometres slightly north-west of An Caisteal.

Glen Falloch from An Caisteal

5
An Caisteal

Pronunciation: *Ann Kas-chaal*
Meaning: the castle
Height: 995m (3264ft); Rank: 147
OS Landranger Maps 50 & 56
Summit grid ref: NN378193 (cairn)

PART of a neat cluster of seven Munros just south of Crianlarich, An Caisteal is accessed easily from a large layby on the A82. Toward its summit is a rocky knoll from which the hill gets its name – the castle.

An Caisteal is usually climbed with its near neighbour – Beinn a' Chroin – the two being linked by a high col at 805m (2641ft) known as the Bealach Buidhe. It's the route I recommend here, giving a nice short day and a pleasing round, but the hill can also be linked with others in the area.

Immediately south-west lies Beinn Chabhair – although it's very close by, including it in the round involves a considerable height loss of more than 300m (1000ft) and some tricky navigation in bad weather on rocky slopes.

In his excellent book *Scotland*, Chris Townsend describes the traverse of all the Crianlarich Munros as one of the best high-level walks in the Highlands, if one of the least well known. It's a considerable undertaking, involving 3375m (11,073ft) of ascent over 26km (16.2 miles) and at least 10 to 12 hours on the hill.

Like its neighbours, An Caisteal consists of steep, grassy lower slopes, with rocky outcrops at the summit. In summer, the lower parts are wonderfully green and lush, but it's a steep, rugged little mountain and the small tor en route to the summit gives a wee bit of scrambling with some quite considerable exposure on the left side.

It was on this hill that I experienced an inversion for the first time – and also saw my first Brocken spectre. I'd only climbed a handful of Munros at the time. It was an incredible feeling, breaking through the thick cloud barrier to leave a land of murk and clag for bright sun and blue skies.

The cloud beneath was like a vast, turbulent white ocean, the summits of the surrounding Munros and hills north to the Blackmount – and beyond to Glencoe and even Ben Nevis – protruding like rocky islands. It left quite an impression.

Beinn Chabhair from An Caisteal

NEAREST TOWN: Crianlarich is around 5km (3.1 miles) north. Although a small village, it has a railway station, several hotels, pubs and a youth hostel. It also has a small corner shop, which has a limited range of outdoor kit, in case you forget anything.

RECOMMENDED ROUTE
Start grid ref: NN368238
Distance: 14.5km (9 miles)
Ascent 1050m (3445ft)
Time: 5hrs

THE ROUTE

Including the neighbouring Munro Beinn a' Chroin makes for a pleasant, relatively short round that involves some minor, fun scrambling.

Start at the large layby on the east side of the A82 – there's space for many cars here. An underpass – or cattle creep – takes you beneath the railway. A track takes you over a bridge and along the left bank of the River Falloch. After roughly 1km (0.6 miles) leave the track and head up the grassy flanks of Sron Gharbh.

A worn path rides over a gnarly ridge – the appropriately named "Twistin Hill". Ahead, the rocky knoll that gives An Caisteal its name seems to bar the way. Most fun is taking it head-on – the exposure on the left side is quite considerable. If you don't fancy that, it is easily bypassed on steep, grassy ground to the right.

From the summit – where views extend to Ben Nevis – follow the south ridge, which becomes increasingly steep and rocky, to the Bealach Buidhe. A clear path zig-zags up the rocky west ridge of Beinn a' Chroin. Some minor – and fun – scrambling

Did You Know?

Crianlarich's name derives from the Gaelic for "low pass" and refers to its importance as a junction of the main routes to the North-West Highlands from the south and east.

BROCKEN SPECTRE

The Brocken spectre takes its name from the Brocken mountain in Germany's Harz range, where the phenomenon was first recorded.

According to the Met Office, they're the magnified shadow of the observer, cast on to clouds or banks of mist.

The sun, shining from behind the observer, throws the shadow through the mist below. Water droplets refract the sun's rays, creating a halo of colour around the shadow, while the movement of the observer, as well as the roiling of the cloud, cause a strange sensation of movement.

The term was coined in the late 18th century by scientist Johann Silberschlag, who spent much of his time in the Harz mountains.

Some believe the spectre is the origin of the legendary Big Grey Man, said to prowl the flanks of Ben Macdui, terrifying unwary walkers.

takes you through crags to the plateau.

East of a small lochan sits a cairn that marks the summit of this Munro at 942m (3091ft). On old maps, the eastern summit is listed as slightly higher – but it's actually 2m (6.5ft) lower. It's a nice viewpoint – and once was regarded as the Munro – so you're as well to take it in.

Backtrack slightly from here, before following the north ridge and then dropping into the glen.

The walk out is very boggy. An interesting feature is a massive boulder with a small jungle growing on top! Pass this and follow the east bank of the River Falloch to pick up the track once more and back to the start.

Beinn Dorain across Auch Gleann, winter

6

Beinn Dorain

THE main trunk road to the north-west, the West Highland Railway and the West Highland Way all pass very close to Beinn Dorain, so the hill's well known to many.

I've climbed it on a few occasions and travelled past it many hundreds of times – but I still thrill at the sight of it.

I love travelling north with someone who catches sight of Beinn Dorain for the first time. As you round the sweeping bend on the A82 north of Tyndrum, the vast bulk of this perfect pyramid of a peak looms into view. Their reaction is invariably "wow!"

From this angle, Beinn Dorain appears conical and almost impossibly steep – a formidable prospect that utterly dominates its surroundings. There's a feeling you've suddenly arrived in the Highlands.

With their big sharp horns, Highland cows can look pretty fearsome, but they're generally big softies really. Beinn Dorain's a bit like that too, and, when approached from Bridge of Orchy, the ascent is much easier than you'd imagine after first seeing the hill.

It's a bit of a pull up to the bealach and beyond, then you follow a lovely long ridge that takes you to the summit.

The hill is one of a group of five fairly tightly packed Munros in this area.

Pronunciation: *Ben Doh-ran*
Meaning: possibly hill of the streamlet
Height: 1076m (3530ft); Rank: 64
OS Landranger Map 50
Summit grid ref: NN325378 (cairn)

Combining Beinn Dorain with its nearest neighbour, Beinn an Dothaidh, makes for a fine day out.

The superfit sometimes climb all five in a day – a truly massive undertaking which needs the long days of summer if you want a chance of finishing in daylight.

A couple of hundred metres shy of the summit lies a considerable cairn, known as Carn Sassunaich, the Sassenach's – or Southerner's – Cairn.

It's not clear how it got its name but one – quite uncharitable – theory has it that in thick mist "daft southerners" might mistake the cairn for the true summit! Whatever the truth of it, the views of the Southern Highlands from the actual summit are wonderful, giving a rarely seen perspective of the Glen Lochay and Glen Lyon hills in particular.

Beinn Dorain and Auch Gleann, summer

NEAREST TOWN: Tyndrum lies just 8km (5 miles) directly south. It's a small settlement at the junction of the A82 and A85 roads. It has a train station, pub, hotel and the famous Green Welly Stop, which sells everything from petrol to outdoor gear. For award-wining fish and chips, visit the Real Food Cafe.

RECOMMENDED ROUTE
Start grid ref: NN300394
Distance: 14km (8.7 miles)
Ascent: 1200m (3937ft)
Time: 6hrs

THE ROUTE

The route – which takes in two Munros, Beinn Dorain and Beinn an Dothaidh – starts at Bridge of Orchy train station, where there is limited parking. Alternatively, there's a large public car park right next to the Bridge of Orchy Hotel on the A82.

From the station, you walk beneath the tracks via the underpass. An obvious path crosses the West Highland Way and heads east into the Coire an Dothaidh.

The going is easy enough, with the odd boggy section – especially lower down. The path steepens toward the bealach between Beinn Dorain and its neighbour, Beinn an Dothaidh. The col is marked by a cairn.

These Munros are so close together and easily climbed from the bealach – it'd be a shame to do just one. I think Beinn Dorain is best left until last. It's such a pleasingly pointed peak that it's the real highlight of this walk.

For Beinn an Dothaidh, follow the clear path north-east, then north to the 1004m (3294ft) summit. The ground drops away steeply from the top and the airy views over Rannoch Moor are wonderful.

From here, take in the south summit before dropping back to the bealach.

Beinn Dorain's summit is a little over 2km (1.2 miles) away, almost directly south. At first the path tackles quite a steep, wide slope before the ridge narrows and becomes more defined.

In poor visibility, bear in mind that the sizeable Carn Sassunaich does not mark the summit. Instead continue a short way to another bealach, before the short pull up to the true summit.

Did You Know?

Renowned Gaelic poet Duncan Ban MacIntyre was a gamekeeper in this part of Scotland. His most famous work is *Moladh Beinn Dobhrain*, or *In Praise of Ben Dorain*.

BEINN DORAIN ORCHESTRA

Beinn Dorain is the only Munro with a choral symphony devoted to it. Scots composer Ronald Stevenson's work in *In Praise of Beinn Dorain* – for full chorus and chamber choir, with chamber and symphony orchestra – received its world premiere in Glasgow City Halls on January 19, 2008.

The work, described at the time as "bold" and "audacious" was performed by the BBC Scottish Symphony Orchestra, the chorus of Scottish Opera, Glasgow University Chapel Choir, the Edinburgh Singers, a chamber orchestra, two child soloists and a tenor.

The piece is based on Duncan Ban MacIntyre's Gaelic poem of the same name, and its translation into English by celebrated Scottish writer Hugh MacDiarmid.

The work was 45 years in the making, with Stevenson having started it in the 1960s. The composer, then in his 80th year, was present at the premiere. Afterwards, the audience cheered him to the rafters.

Beinn an Dothaidh and Loch Tulla

Beinn Achaladair from Gorton Bothy

Beinn Achaladair

7
Beinn Achaladair

THE best view of Beinn Achaladair is from the north, heading down the A82 road from Glen Coe.

It forms, with its eastern neighbour Beinn a' Chreachain and Beinn an Dothaidh in the west, a great wall along the southern limits of Rannoch Moor.

One of five Munros in the Bridge of Orchy area, it's most usually climbed from Achallader Farm. From here, a there-and-back into Coire Achaladair will give a straightforward and relatively short day.

A far better outing is to climb the hill along with Beinn a' Chreachain. As a pair, not only do Munro-baggers get two hills ticked, but you'll enjoy what I reckon is the best walk of the Orchy Munros.

Doing them clockwise means quite a long approach up the Water of Tulla to reach Beinn a' Chreachain, but it takes you through Crannach Wood, an area of beautiful native pine and birch forest.

The wood becomes quite open, and I remember the first time I walked here we were tracked by a fox high on the flank of the hill. It followed us for miles. Later, once we'd gained height, we followed fox tracks in the snow, which led right over the summit.

The ridge itself is a superb high-level walk. It's well defined and at times narrow

Pronunciation: *Ben Acha-lat-ter*
Meaning: hill of the field of hard water
Height: 1038m (3406ft); Rank: 94
OS Landranger Map 50
Summit grid ref: NN344432

with one or two wee rocky steps – it's never difficult though.

Ahead are incredible views of Loch Tulla, the Blackmount and the hills beyond, receding into the distance in layers of shade.

The farmer at Achallader has built a large parking area at the entrance to the farm, just east of the A82.

The walk in takes you past the farm buildings. They include the ruins of a great stone tower. It's the remains of one of the seven castles of Black Duncan of Cowal, Campbell of Glenorchy. It was built in the 1590s to guard a cattle-droving route through to Glen Lyon.

The ruins are significant as, in February 1692, it was here that Robert Campbell rested with his Government troops as they made their way to Glen Coe – where they were to commit the infamous atrocity we now know as the Massacre of Glen Coe.

NEAREST TOWN: Tyndrum is 13km (8.1 miles) south. The small settlement at the junction of the A82 and A85 has two train stations, a pub, hotel, caravan and camping site and the famous Green Welly Stop, which sells everything from petrol to outdoor gear. For award-wining fish and chips, visit the Real Food Cafe.

RECOMMENDED ROUTE
Start grid ref: NN313437
Distance: 21km (13.1 miles)
Ascent: 1200m (3937ft)
Time: 7hrs

THE ROUTE

A large parking area has been built a short distance along the entrance track to Achallader Farm.

From the farm, a track – the old right of way to Rannoch – is followed. It fords the Allt Ur – if the river's in spate, there is a bridge just upstream of the farm.

The track continues to the old bridge over the Water of Tulla, where the path forks. One branch continues along the south bank of the river and through Crannach Wood. It can be boggy but the woodland is lovely.

The alternative crosses the river and continues for several kilometres on the Land Rover track to a footbridge that leads you back into the woods.

At the time of writing, the old bridge is down and the crossing would be very difficult in times of spate, so I'd recommend sticking to the south bank.

The path leads you through the ancient forest, to a footbridge over the rail tracks. Then follow the tracks until you meet a river – the Allt Coire an Lochain. Leave the railway and follow the stream into Coire an Lochain. Head east from here on easy slopes to reach the ridge of Beinn a' Chreachain, just right of Pt 961m.

A twisting ridge – which could be tricky in poor visibility – leads to the 1081m (3547ft) summit. Descend north-west a

Gorton Bothy

Did You Know?

The ruined tower at Achallader Farm was one of seven castles built by Black Duncan of Cowal, Campbell of Glenorchy. Dating from the 1590s, it was later burned down by Jacobites following the 1692 Glen Coe Massacre.

short distance to flatter ground which then begins climbing south-west over Meall Buidhe. The route continues south-west to a col before Beinn Achaladair. The route up the Munro is steep and rocky in sections.

From the summit, traverse over the south top and continue to the bealach with Beinn an Dothaidh. From here, head north into the corrie and back to Achallader Farm.

Beinn an Dothaidh from Beinn Achaladair

A "BUT AND BEN" BOTHY

Gorton Bothy is ideally situated for an ascent of Beinn Achaladair.

Found at grid reference NN375481 it's 8km (5 miles) along forestry roads from the A82. It's easily cycle-able from the car park west of Achallader Farm. A good option is heading in on an evening, staying overnight, then ascending the hill the following morning.

The two-room bothy is a typical "but and ben"-style building. It was once a shepherd's home, occupied well into the 1950s by a Mr Charlie Murray and his family.

Nearby was a rail-halt for the West Highland Line, and the cottage was a meeting point for nearby farming communities, where they brought their sheep for onward transport. The halt included a small platform, a signal box and even a school housed in an old railway carriage.

Today, other than the cottage, all that remains is a pile of stones and bricks. The Mountain Bothies Association has cared for the building since 1978.

Stob Binnein and Stob Coire an Lochain

Stob a' Chroin above Inverlochlarig

Did You Know?

Stob Binnein and its near neighbour Ben More form a distinctive outline and are visible for such a great distance that they're sometimes referred to as "Castor and Pollux", the twins of classical mythology.

8
Stob Binnein

IMMEDIATELY north of the Trossachs, Stob Binnein lies at the heart of a beautiful, compact area of fabulously rugged little hills and sparkling lochs.

It's classic Rob Roy country, and the legendary outlaw was born, lived and died among these hills. His grave lies in Balquhidder churchyard, which you'll pass on the road in if you follow my recommended route.

Stob Binnein is most usually climbed with its partner, the slightly higher Ben More, from the A85 roadside near Crianlarich. It's the easiest route for bagging both hills, but the initial ascent up Ben More is punishing.

By far the best way to climb Stob Binnein, at least, is from the end of the minor road at Inverlochlarig Farm. The route can be extended to take in Ben More, but it means re-ascending Stob Binnein to get back to the car park. As a single hill from here, Stob Binnein is a fine choice for a short winter's day – providing the winding single-track road is clear of ice.

Tackling the hill from here gives a real flavour of the area, which I don't think you get approaching from the north.

It's not terribly far from the Central Belt – Stirling is barely 55 km (34 miles) away – but it feels far more remote, probably as a result of the 14km (8.7-mile) drive along

Pronunciation: *Stob Bin-yin*
Meaning: possibly conical peak, or peak of the anvil
Height: 1165m (3822ft); Rank: 18
OS Landranger Map 51
Summit grid ref: NN434227 (cairn)

twisting single track to get to Inverlochlarig from the A84.

It's picture-postcard Scotland, and the area teems with history. Wildlife you're likely to encounter includes red deer and golden eagles.

In summer in particular, I find the area quite breathtaking. The hills and glens are so lush and verdant and alive. It's wonderful.

A friend of mine, Alex MacLennan, a Lewisman, often uses an old Gaelic saying in high summer, *tha am feur gorm,* which literally means *the grass is blue.* I never quite got it until one hot July day in the hills around Inverlochlarig – with the undergrowth so rich and the sun burning in a clear azure sky, grassy hillsides here do take on a blue tinge through the heat haze. The grass is so green it's blue!

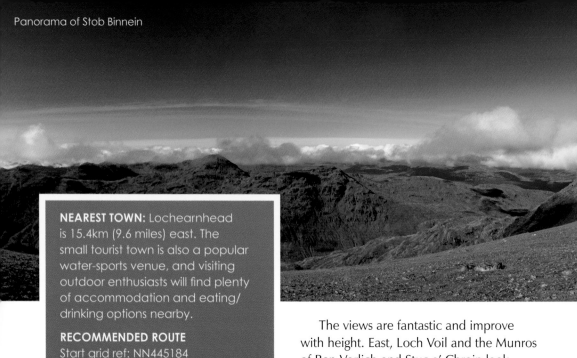

NEAREST TOWN: Lochearnhead is 15.4km (9.6 miles) east. The small tourist town is also a popular water-sports venue, and visiting outdoor enthusiasts will find plenty of accommodation and eating/drinking options nearby.

RECOMMENDED ROUTE
Start grid ref: NN445184
Distance: 8km (5 miles)
Ascent: 1050m (3445ft)
Time: 4.5hrs

THE ROUTE

There's a decent-sized parking area at the end of the public road about 0.8km (0.5 miles) shy of Inverlochlarig Farm, with information boards and a shelter – handy for getting changed in at the end of a day in bad weather.

From here, cross the road to a stile over a dry-stone wall. The stile has a familiar green ScotWays sign pointing the way to Stob Binnein. There's no real doubt about the route though . . . up.

The initial section heads north on brutally steep grass slopes to Stob Invercarnaig. Once the ridge is gained, the going becomes much more pleasant.

The views are fantastic and improve with height. East, Loch Voil and the Munros of Ben Vorlich and Stuc a' Chroin look magnificent. South, rugged green Corbetts give way to the rumpled land of the Trossachs.

The gentle ridge takes you to Stob Coire an Lochain, then there's a slight descent before a steeper climb to Stob Binnein's summit.

Ben More, just a couple of kilometres north, is tempting. It's the higher summit, at 1174m (3852ft) but Stob Binnein, with its conical summit perched atop its ridges, is by far the finer hill. The views north from here are extensive – much of the Southern and Central Highlands is visible.

This grand pair of Munros form an unmistakable outline and are visible from many miles away – I've seen them from as far as Beinn Bhrotain in the Cairngorms.

The easiest route back to the start is to retrace your steps.

Did You Know?

Nearby, on the northern shore of Loch Voil, is a Buddhist retreat centre. The Dhanakosa Centre was once a hotel, but retreats have been held there since 1992.

AN INFAMOUS OUTLAW

Inverlochlarig Farm was once the home of the infamous outlaw Rob Roy MacGregor.

It was here that he died on December 28, 1734, peacefully, aged 63, in his bed, which is perhaps a surprise given his adventurous and often troubled life during a very turbulent time in Scottish and British history.

There's a story that, while Rob was on his deathbed at Inverlochlarig, an old rival wished to visit and make his peace. Rob insisted on being dressed, complete with sword and daggers, lest it ever be said an enemy saw him on his sickbed.

Once the man departed, Rob – exhausted – returned to his bed for the last time and asked his piper to strike up his favourite tune.

His grave, a short distance away at Balquidder churchyard, is a popular tourist spot.

Cruach Ardrain from Stob Binnein

Loch Doine and Loch Voil from Stob Inverlochlarig

Ben Lui from Glen Cononish

Looking towards Ben Lui

9
Ben Lui

WITH elegant lines and an alpine-like grace, Ben Lui is considered one of the most beautiful mountains in the Southern Highlands, if not all Scotland.

It's the tallest peak in a line of four – Beinn a' Chleibh, Ben Lui, Ben Oss and Beinn Dubhchraig – that zig-zags east to west from between Tyndrum and Crianlarich.

Although its neighbours are also Munros, they're far smaller than Ben Lui, and the fine mountain appears to stand alone – a proud pyramid visible and well known from many other peaks, some a considerable distance away. It's a landmark of the Southern Highlands.

The hill looks its best when approached from the north-east, from Dalrigh, from where its most distinctive feature, the great bowl of Coire Gaothaich, is clearly visible.

This corrie usually holds snow late into summer, when all around is a verdant, vivid green, lending the mountain even more of an alpine aspect.

Easy access by railway meant Ben Lui was a hill popular with Scotland's mountaineering pioneers in the Victorian era. Coire Gaothaich holds a number of lower-grade winter routes for climbers. Most famous is Central Gully, first climbed in 1892.

> Pronunciation: *Ben Loo-ay*
> Meaning: hill of the calf
> Height: 1130m (3707ft); Rank: 27
> OS Landranger Map: 50
> Summit grid ref: NN266263

The Central Gully is a Grade 1 but in a thrilling situation and feels much more adventurous. It pops you right out on the summit. However, there can be a considerable cornice at the top of the route, and the gully is prone to avalanche.

The quickest way up the hill is from the north-west, the Glen Lochay side. There's a car park off the south side of the A85 at NN239278. It involves an awkward river crossing and there's the railway to negotiate. You're required to go beneath it – crossing the rails risks your life and a hefty trespass fine. The underpass also contains a stream, so you're likely to get your feet wet.

After that, it's a steep slog up grassy slopes. Hardly an inspiring route for such a majestic hill. Taking in the adjacent Beinn a' Chleibh – and it's hard to credit this is a Munro when seen next to Ben Lui – gives a route of roughly 10km (6.2 miles), with 1100m (3609ft) of ascent and should take just four or five hours.

Far better for those who like a bit of scrambling is the longer route – and

NEAREST TOWN: Tyndrum lies just 7.5km (4.7 miles) north-east. The small settlement at the junction of the A82 and A85 has two train stations, a pub, hotel, caravan and camping site and the famous Green Welly Stop, which sells everything from petrol to outdoor gear. For award-wining fish and chips, visit the Real Food Cafe.

RECOMMENDED ROUTE
Start grid ref: NN343291
Distance: 18.5km (11.5 miles)
Ascent: 1150m (3773ft)
Time: 7hrs

the one I recommend – from Dalrigh via Cononish. Much of the way can be cycled, saving a lot of time.

THE ROUTE

There's a large parking area at Dalrigh, just south of Tyndrum on the A82.

The West Highland Way passes here, and you share the route briefly.

An excellent private road leads west, eventually reaching – and then following – the north bank of the River Cononish.

About 1.5km (0.9 miles) before the farm at Cononish, another private road merges from the north – this leads from Tyndrum and is an alternative start point.

The road and track can be cycled far beyond the farm and will save lots of time if an option. The glen beyond the farm is the site of the gold-mine workings. Sadly, it doesn't make for the prettiest of sections – but the grand, towering north-east face of Ben Lui is what will draw the eye. It's a majestic sight.

The track ends at the Allt an Rund. Pick up a path here that leads uphill into Coire Gaothaich. At a more level section, strike north-west up much steeper ground, aiming for Ben Lui's north-east ridge.

On the ridge, the route becomes steep

and narrow. It's a wonderful way up a beautiful hill. The scrambling is simple and ends quite suddenly at the Munro's north-west top. A short traverse over easy ground takes you to the summit.

It should be noted that, although a relatively undemanding scramble in summer conditions, this can be quite a testing route when snow and ice are lying. And this high on Ben Lui, those winter conditions can easily extend into late April and May. Appropriate equipment and experience are needed.

The easiest return is by the same route.

Did You Know?

Ben Lui's most dramatic feature, the great scoop known as Coire Gaothaich, translates as "the corrie of the winds".

The River Cononish from Ben Lui

BEN LUI GOLDMINES

A controversial gold mine at Cononish, at the foot of Ben Lui, was granted full planning permission in February 2018.

It's the first commercial gold mine in Scotland, and was given the green light after a site visit by Loch Lomond and The Trossachs National Park planning committee.

The plans divided opinion – Mountaineering Scotland objected to the proposals, but the local Strathfillan community group was supportive.

Operators Scotgold Resources aim to mine more than 500,000 tonnes of ore over a 17-year period. The company plans to invest £500,000 in the local community and says as many as 52 jobs could be created.

A temporary bridge will be built to keep mine traffic away from walkers on the West Highland Way long-distance route from Milngavie to Fort William.

An earlier trial saw the mine produce gold for the first time in August 2016.

Cruach Ardrain from Beinn a' Chroin

Beinn Tulaichean from Cruach Ardrain

10
Cruach Ardrain

ITS distinctive, rugged outline ensures rocky Cruach Ardrain is a hill familiar in outline far and wide.

There's a wee hill I climb often, for training, just north of my home in the Trossachs. The view from the summit is a wonderful panorama, a great ring of peaks from Ben Lomond in the west, then Ben Venue, on to Beinn Tulaichean, Cruach Ardrain, Stob Binnein, Ben More, all the way round to Benvane and Ben Ledi in the east.

For me, it's craggy Cruach Ardrain that steals the show. It's far smaller than its immediate neighbours – towering Ben More and Stob Binnein, both aesthetically pleasing hills – but Cruach Ardrain's steep, broken north-eastern aspect gives it real drama.

It lies at the heart of the seven Munros just south of Crianlarich – and of the five western Munros in that group, it's easily the finest summit.

The hill is often climbed along with the smaller Munro Beinn Tulaichean, which lies about 2km (1.2 miles) away at the southern tip of Cruach Ardrain's south ridge. They don't really feel like separate hills.

A common way of climbing them is from Inverlochlarig, at the end of a long section of single-track road from Balquhidder off the A84.

It's a bit of a slog up steep grass and not the best way up the hills. I reckon the

Pronunciation: *Croo-ach Ar-dren*
Meaning: Stack of the high peaks
Height: 1046m (3432ft); Rank: 87
OS Landranger Maps 50, 51 & 56
Summit grid ref: NN409212 (cairn)

approach from the Crianlarich side is much nicer – it gives you the chance to better appreciate the rough character of the hill. And you can always add on Beinn Tulaichean as a there-and-back if you've time.

Ascent from the Crianlarich side is a particularly fine winter outing for experienced mountaineers. In fact there are even some graded routes for climbers, probably the best-known being Y Gully, a winter Grade 1.

You can turn the route into a bit of a horseshoe by carrying on from the summit to the Munro top Stob Garbh – the initial part of this is very rocky and steep and requires great care, particularly when icy.

An Caisteal from Cruach Ardrain

NEAREST TOWN: Crianlarich is around 5km (3 miles) north-west. Although a small village, it has a railway station, several hotels, pubs and a youth hostel. It also has a small corner shop, with a limited range of outdoor kit.

RECOMMENDED ROUTE
Start grid ref: NN368238
Distance: 10km (6.2 miles)
Ascent: 1000m (3281ft)
Time: 5hrs

THE ROUTE

The best starting place is the large layby off the A82, immediately south of Crianlarich.

From here, duck under the railway via the cattle creep and follow the track along the River Falloch for about 1km (0.6 miles). Down on your left is a bridge over the river.

Heading north-west up grassy slopes for 1km (0.6 miles) takes you on to the ridge that leads first over Grey Height and then Meall Dhamh.

The path is clear but eroded. After this minor summit you lose a wee bit of height before a stiff climb up to Cruach Ardrain's summit.

Before the summit proper is a flatter area, with two cairns a short distance apart. The actual summit lies north-east of here. While it could be confusing in mist, the real summit cairn, however, is unmistakable – it's large, and sits on rock perched airily over craggy ground. It's a tremendous viewpoint. You're just into the Highlands here – the Central Belt is barely an hour's drive away. All around is mountainous country and it feels wild.

The route stats above assume you'll retrace your steps – but there are other options. A second Munro, Beinn Tulaichean, lies roughly 1.5km (0.9 miles) along Cruach Ardrain's south ridge and only involves a drop-off of about 120m (400ft).

Tyndrum Hills from Cruach Ardrain

Another option is to continue on to the north-west top, Stob Garbh. The descent from the summit requires care, and the route to the top is over an ill-defined ridge.

Once over Stob Garbh, continue along the ridge for about 0.5km (0.3 miles) before heading north-west into Coire Ardrain. Then it's a case of traversing below Grey Height to the bottom of the ridge used in your initial approach.

Beinn a' Chroin from Beinn Tulaichean

NAISMITH'S RULE

Walkers and mountaineers the world over are familiar with Naismith's rule – the formula used to give a rough timing for how long a route should take.

It was devised by Scottish mountaineer William W. Naismith in 1892, while he was traversing Cruach Ardrain on his way to Ben More.

It's been tweaked slightly over the years – and assumes a fairly decent level of fitness – but it's pretty accurate and a useful planning tool. The rule of thumb is to allow one hour for every 5km (3.1 miles) going forward, and an additional hour for every 600m (2000ft) of ascent.

Naismith was a founder member of the Scottish Mountaineering Club and a noted climber with many first ascents. In 1894, he was the first to climb Ben Nevis's Tower Ridge – and thus, as tradition dictates, was given the honour of naming the route.

Ben Lawers Massif from Meall Garbh summit

CENTRAL
HIGHLANDS

Beinn a' Ghlò

▲ Schiehallion

Pitlochry

Aberfeldy

Blairgowrie
and Rattray

Dunkeld

Scone

Ben Lawers

Beinn Ghlas

11
Ben Lawers

SCOTLAND'S 10th highest Munro gives its name to the nature reserve that surrounds it and is famed as the home of some of the rarest alpine plants in the UK.

The mountain and surrounding land – which includes another six Munros – was bought by the National Trust for Scotland in 1950. Known as the Ben Lawers National Nature Reserve, it's an area popular with botanists as well as hillwalkers.

Flora includes saxifrage, alpine forget-me-not and net-leaved willow, among many more – there are over 500 types of lichen alone.

The beauty of the plants is best appreciated in spring and early summer, when the hillsides are alive with flowers in bloom.

For many years, an unsightly NTS visitor centre marred the hillside. It's thankfully been demolished and the land reinstated. The car park remains – although it has been redeveloped and is far more sympathetic to its surroundings. It does, however, sit at around 450m (1476ft) – giving one of the highest start points in the country for Munro-baggers.

Such a high start means an ascent of Ben Lawers, by traversing its neighbouring Munro Beinn Ghlas, is also easily doable on a short winter day. However, the twisting

Pronunciation: *Ben Law-ers*
Meaning: hill of the loud stream, or hill of the claw
Height: 1214m (3983ft); Rank: 10
OS Landranger Map 51
Summit grid ref: NN635414 (trig point & view indicator)

single-track road from the shores of Loch Tay isn't treated in winter, so it's not always possible to drive to the car park.

Ben Lawers played an important role in the development of the skiing industry in Scotland. It was very nearly home to the first skiing centre, until developers looked further north, to areas that hold snow longer than Ben Lawers' northern corries. It remains, however, an area very popular with ski-tourers.

Ben Lawers was first accurately measured in Victorian times and the fact that it fell just short of the 4000ft mark caused great disappointment – only nine hills in Scotland are in this bracket. One local man – Malcolm Ferguson – was so dismayed he paid for an enormous 20ft cairn to be built on top of the mountain, to get the summit over the prized height. Little now remains of its presence.

THE ROUTE

This straightforward route heads over the Munro Beinn Ghlas en route to the summit of mighty Ben Lawers.

Cross the road from the National Trust for Scotland car park and follow the path into an area fenced off from deer and sheep. Entry is through a large gate.

Given their proximity to the Central Belt, these are enormously popular hills and a clear path heads over both summits.

Much work has been done on the path by landowners the NTS to reduce erosion.

Keep to the main path, which heads alongside the Burn of Edramucky. After around 1km (0.6 miles), the route takes you up grassy slopes on to the south ridge of Beinn Ghlas, which takes you to the summit.

The top is marked by a small heap of stones at the high point of the ridge. To the north, the ground falls away quite dramatically. It doesn't, however, really feel like a summit. Ahead, the soaring summit of Ben Lawers dominates and Beinn Ghlas's top can just feel like another bump in the ridge. I suspect some walkers won't even be aware they've climbed a Munro!

The route heads north-east to a high, wide bealach at almost 1000m (3281ft). The walking's easy and pleasant. From here, a steeper grassy slope quickly takes you to the summit.

Meall Corrianaich

The views from such a high point are extensive – west is Glen Coe and all the big hills of the Central Highlands, and to the north, Ben Macdui and the Cairngorms are visible on a clear day.

It's possible to combine these hills with others in the area, such as An Stuc, for a longer day. Alternatively, simply retrace your steps back to the car park.

Beinn Ghlas from Ben Lawers

CRANNOG

One of the non-hill highlights of this area is The Scottish Crannog Centre, near Kenmore at the head of Loch Tay.

It's a modern reconstruction of a crannog – a house built on stilts or an artificial island in prehistoric times.

The crannog was built as an archaeological experiment in the mid 1990s using, as far as was possible, ancient techniques. It's a reconstruction of a nearby crannog that dated from around 500 BC and which has been extensively excavated. The dark, cold water and peaty loch bed allowed for incredible preservation of artefacts – finds included a 2500-year-old wooden butter dish that still contained butter.

The crannog is open to visitors during the tourist season. It's a thatched building constructed on stilts and linked to the shore by a causeway.

There's evidence of some 18 crannogs around the loch.

Stuchd an Lochain and Lochan nan Cat in Glen Lyon

Did You Know?

The dammed loch on the shores of which lies Stuchd an Lochain is called Loch an Daimh, which translates as the "loch of the stag".

View from the summit of Stuchd an Lochain

12
Stuchd an Lochain

FEW hills in the Central Highlands feel as remote as Stuchd an Lochain. The hill rises above Loch an Daimh, deep along Glen Lyon. It's hidden up an offshoot of the minor road that runs the length of the glen to Loch Lyon.

Vehicle access to the glen from the east is from Fortingall. From the south, the Ben Lawers road that runs from the north shore of Loch Tay takes you eventually to Bridge of Balgie, where it meets the Glen Lyon road.

Both routes are along twisting, narrow single track that take an age to negotiate – far longer than the distance would at first suggest.

It's ironic then, given the effort to get there, that Stuchd an Lochain presents one of the quickest ascents of any Munro. The Giorra Dam, at which you park, lies at 410m (1345ft) above sea level – so almost half the hard work is already done.

Even in winter – assuming you're first able to get to the hill along untreated roads – an ascent shouldn't take much longer than 3.5 hours. As a result, many baggers include an ascent of Meall Buidhe, which lies on the north side of the loch and is also accessed from the dam. The two together make a hill day, more or less.

Stuchd an Lochain – like any Munro – shouldn't be underestimated though,

Pronunciation: *Stooch-k an Lochan*
Meaning: peak of the little loch
Height: 960m (3150ft); Rank: 197
OS Landranger Map 51
Summit grid ref: NN483448 (cairn)

especially in winter conditions. The initial slopes are pretty steep, and there's another very steep section to climb to Pt 888 on Creag an Fheadain. I climbed the hill one April and the ice was pretty solid here – I was glad of my crampons and axe.

The best feature of the Munro is the beautiful little Lochan nan Cat that nestles in its northern corrie and gives the hill its name. The summit perches airily on crags directly above the lochan.

My own favourite view of the hill is from quite a distance away – from the A82 on Rannoch Moor. As you head south on the road and the Munros of Beinn an Dothaidh, Beinn Achaladair and Beinn a' Chreachain loom into view, just to their left is Stuchd an Lochain, a graceful, low-angled and perfectly symmetrical pyramid.

Loch an Daimh and Meall Buidh from the summit of Stuchd an Lochain

NEAREST TOWN: Killin's the closest "big" town. It lies about 15km (9.3 miles) south-east. It has a variety of places to eat and drink, shops – including an outdoor store and supermarket – plus accommodation from holiday parks to hotels.

RECOMMENDED ROUTE
Start grid ref: NN511463
Distance: 9km (5.6 miles)
Ascent: 715m (2346ft)
Time: 3.5hrs

THE ROUTE

From the Giorra Dam, head south on the track that curves along the shore of the loch.

After about 150–200m you'll find a rough path on the left. A cairn marks the spot but the path itself is very obvious.

It contours the hillside initially, before then swinging almost directly uphill. It's very steep in sections, badly eroded and quite mucky in wetter weather.

The ridge is gained at cairn, from where a line of old fence posts leads across a very short, easier – and drier – section, before the steep pull on to Creag an Fheadain.

82

The summit of Stuchd an Lochain

Did You Know?

Sir Walter Scott referred to Glen Lyon as "the longest, loneliest and loveliest glen in Scotland".

Head south-west from here, over a slight dip, before a sharp wee climb to Sron a' Chona Choirein.

Head west, around the rim of the corrie – views down into the little Lochan nan Cat, an almost perfect circle, are lovely.

A brief climb takes you to the summit, with its cairn sitting grandly above steep crags.

On a clear day, Ben Nevis is clearly visible beyond Rannoch Moor.

The easiest descent is to retrace your steps – perhaps ascending Meall Buidhe from the dam if you've time. An even more pleasing route is to continue west over the 837m (2746ft) Corbett Sron a' Choire Chnapanich. Continue the circuit of Loch an Daimh over Meall Cruinn and the Munro Meall Buidhe, 932m (3058ft). The entire circuit is about 20km (12.4 miles) with 1000m (3281ft) of ascent.

MAD COLIN CAMPBELL

Stuchd an Lochain has a claim to have the first recorded Munro ascent in Scotland – 300 years before the concept of Munros was devised!

Author Ronald Turnbull, in his book *Walking Highland Perthshire*, tells of how, in 1590, local laird Mad Colin Campbell of Meggernie climbed the hill with his faithful ghillie.

However Mad Colin, or *Cailean Gorach* in Gaelic, wasn't interested in bagging peaks; rather he wanted to chase a herd of wild goats off the summit cliffs to their deaths in Lochan nan Cat below.

Not content with killing goats, Mad Colin is said to have then ordered his ghillie to leap from the cliffs. The poor man asked he be allowed to kneel to pray first – and then pushed Colin over the edge when his boss turned his back!

Cameron McNeish also recounts the tale in his book *The Munros*.

Schiehallion reflected in Loch Rannoch

Loch Rannoch from Schiehallion

Did You Know?

To celebrate the end of his experiments on Schiehallion, Maskelyne invited locals to a party on the summit. It was a pretty wild do – the fiddler set fire to his instrument and the summit observatory burned down!

13
Schiehallion

ITS shape, location, name, folklore and history all combine to make Schiehallion one of Scotland's most iconic mountains.

It's a lonely peak, unconnected to any others. From the south particularly, it's a broad whaleback of a hill – but from other vantage points, especially across Loch Rannoch and the north-west, it's wonderfully conical in shape, like the perfect mountain from a child's picture book.

Schiehallion's isolation, stature and unmistakable profile make it one of the easiest mountains to identify. Indeed, given its position in almost the dead centre of the country, probably no hill is as visible from as many other hills as Schiehallion.

The mountain's isolation and highly regular shape meant it was the ideal location for experiments in the late 18th century to measure the mass of the Earth. It was during this work that the concept of contour lines was developed – something for which all hillwalkers, climbers and ramblers owe a debt of gratitude.

The romance of its name – Schiehallion, the fairy hill of the Caledonians – lends the hill a mystique that alone is enough to draw visitors to its flanks.

The upper part of the mountain consists of hard white quartzite. The lower parts are limestone and contain many caves –

Pronunciation: *Shee-hally-yan*
Meaning: fairy hill of the Caledonians
Height: 1083m (3553ft); Rank: 59
OS Landranger Map 51
Summit grid ref: NN713547 (small cairn)

particularly on the southern slopes.

There are many myths and legends associated with the mountain and its caverns. One – Uamh Tom a' Mhor-fhir, or Cave of the Hill of the Big Man – was said to be the entrance to the land of the fairies.

It's no surprise such an interesting hill is also a very popular one. Whatever time of year you climb it, you're likely to have company.

With easy access, a good car park at Braes of Foss and an excellent path most of the way up, Schiehallion is a straightforward, relatively easy Munro.

The upper part of the hill, however, is a massive boulder field consisting of huge rocks – it can make the going quite tough.

The summit has a small cairn perched on a rocky outcrop and the views are immense – a short distance north-east lies Beinn a' Ghlò. Even more impressive is the view west, to the dramatic peaks of Glen Coe, rising sharply beyond the flat, watery expanse of Rannoch Moor.

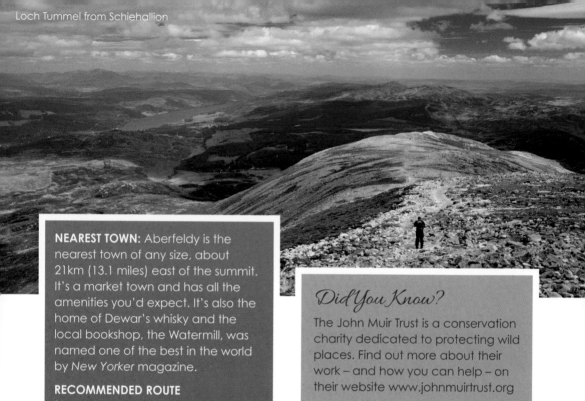

NEAREST TOWN: Aberfeldy is the nearest town of any size, about 21km (13.1 miles) east of the summit. It's a market town and has all the amenities you'd expect. It's also the home of Dewar's whisky and the local bookshop, the Watermill, was named one of the best in the world by *New Yorker* magazine.

RECOMMENDED ROUTE
Start grid ref: NN753556
Distance: 10km (6 miles)
Ascent: 760m (2493ft)
Time: 4hrs

THE ROUTE

Shapely Schiehallion – try saying that after a few – can be climbed from pretty much any direction, with crags and outcrops on the flanks easily avoided.

However, the route I'd recommend is from the Braes of Foss car park on the excellent path constructed by the John Muir Trust a few years ago.

Prior to this work, the route from here up this enormously popular hill had worn an ugly, wide scar on the landscape. It was muddy, steep, slippery and badly eroded.

Did You Know?
The John Muir Trust is a conservation charity dedicated to protecting wild places. Find out more about their work – and how you can help – on their website www.johnmuirtrust.org

The Trust bought the eastern side of the mountain, including the summit, in 1999. They subsequently spent around £800,000 on the new path, which follows an older line up the hill, and have also undertaken lots of work to restore the old route. In time it should heal leaving no trace.

The path leaves Braes of Foss and heads up Schiehallion's long east ridge. It's not waymarked, but the route's simple to follow. The superb track makes going easy and the ascent is quick, the views improving as height is gained.

The track ends at a large cairn roughly at the start of the enormous summit boulder field. The walking here becomes very rough, the route twisting among and over massive quartzite rocks and boulders – care should be taken, and this stony section seems to go on much longer than you first expect.

I think this section of the walk is far more pleasant in late winter or spring, when the angular boulders are buried under a decent covering of consolidated snow. If you're a winter walker, with the appropriate equipment and experience, this is a great choice for a short day.

Simply reverse the route to return to the car park, on the JMT path.

Some walkers don't like such prescribed, maintained routes, the feeling being perhaps that constructed paths make access too easy and detract from the "wildness" of an area.

While that's a view with which I have some sympathy – certainly in our more remote areas – on a hill as popular as this, it's just not practical.

The damage and erosion caused by many thousands of feet is clear to see on too many of our hills. Here, the JMT have put a lot of money and work into restoring the land on the flank of this iconic mountain – we should support their efforts by sticking to the path.

Dun Coillich from Schiehallion

THE SCHIEHALLION EXPERIMENT

For 17 rain-soaked weeks through the summer of 1774, Astronomer Royal Nevil Maskelyne lived in a bothy on Schiehallion as he attempted to calculate the mountain's mass, and thus determine the density of the Earth.

Today, it's known as the Maskelyne, or Schiehallion, Experiment. It involved carefully measuring the mountain to work out what proportion of the Earth it represented – this could be done as the circumference of the planet was already known. Schiehallion was selected as its regular shape meant it was relatively easy to measure.

Charles Hutton was the man charged with measuring the mountain's volume. He worked out it was easier to first measure regularly shaped "slices" of the mountain, and add their volumes together. These slices became the contour lines familiar to all hillwalkers today.

The mass of the mountain was worked out using pendulums, as the gravitational pull of the hill tugged a plumb weight slightly out of true. Using this angle to calculate the mass of the hill, it was then a case of extrapolating the figure to give the density of the Earth.

The figures were pretty accurate – 4500kgm^{-3}. Today it's recorded as 5515kgm.

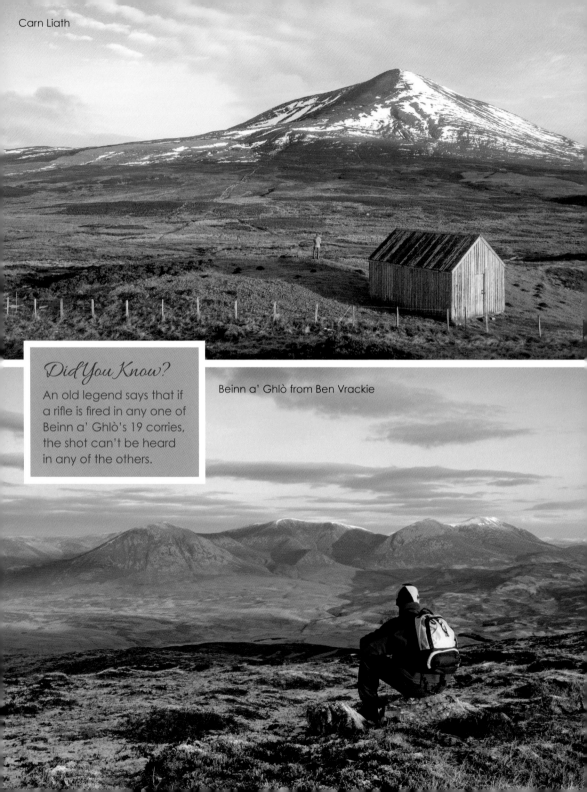

Carn Liath

Beinn a' Ghlò from Ben Vrackie

Did You Know?

An old legend says that if a rifle is fired in any one of Beinn a' Ghlò's 19 corries, the shot can't be heard in any of the others.

14
Carn Liath (Beinn a' Ghlò)

WHEN Carn Liath looms into view shortly after passing Pitlochry while heading north on the A9, it feels like you're about to enter the "real" Highlands.

It's the start of the southern Cairngorms and the first of the really big hills north of Perth. Carn Liath is one of the three Munros that make up Beinn a' Ghlò – which is more mini-mountain range than mountain. The other Munros are Braigh Coire Chruinn-bhalgain and Carn nan Gabhar.

Immediately north is beautiful Glen Tilt, and beyond there the remote hills around Tarf Water. South is Ben Vrackie, the Corbett above Pitlochry, the summit of which offers fine views of Beinn a' Ghlò.

Although Carn Liath is the smallest of the three Munros, for many – being so visible from the A9 – it's the "face" of Beinn a' Ghlò. The higher peaks are hidden further north and west from this angle.

It's also the easiest to access and the quickest to climb – a brief up-and-down from the road end at Loch Moraig.

But it's not the best way to enjoy the hill. Far better is the traverse of all three Munros – it's a big day but another of Scotland's hillwalking "classics". Pick your weather day and it's sure to live long in

Pronunciation: *Carn Lee-ah (Ben a Glow)*; Meaning: grey cairn
Height: 975m (3199ft); Rank: 181
OS Landranger Map 43
Summit grid ref: NN936698 (cairn)

the memory – Beinn a' Ghlò is widely considered the best of the southern Cairngorm hills along with Lochnagar.

Sadly, one of Carn Liath's most obvious features is the wide, eroded scar of a footpath that mars its south-western slope. It's the result of many thousands of boots treading the slopes over decades and is visible from a considerable distance.

Thankfully, at the time of writing, fundraising is underway to repair this damage and construct a new route. The British Mountaineering Council – working with Mountaineering Scotland and the Outdoor Access Trust for Scotland – is seeking to raise £1 million in a campaign called Mend Our Mountains. The cash will be used to repair paths in the UK's national parks. In Scotland, Carn Liath is the hill selected from the Cairngorms National Park. Ben Vane, in Loch Lomond and The Trossachs National Park, will also be worked on.

NEAREST TOWN: The village Blair Atholl is about 8km (5 miles) south-west. It has accommodation, a campsite, garage and selection of shops and places to eat. The spectacular Blair Castle is home to the UK's only private army, the Atholl Highlanders.

RECOMMENDED ROUTE
Start grid ref: NN905670
Distance: 21km (13.1 miles)
Ascent: 1350m (4429ft)
Time: 9hrs

THE ROUTE

As well as Carn Liath, my recommended route takes in the two other Beinn a' Ghlò Munros – Braigh Coire Chruinn-bhalgain and Carn nan Gabhar, which translate as "height of the corrie of round blisters" and "hill of the goats" respectively.

The usual route up Beinn a' Ghlò starts near Loch Moraig, from the car park/layby at the end of the narrow Monzie road that winds its way out of Blair Atholl.

A track leads to Carn Liath, and the eroded path up the slopes leaves no doubt as to the route. The extensive grey screes

on the summit dome give the hill its name.

With much of the day's ascent quickly out the way, what lies ahead is a fantastic, high-level walk. A wonderful, twisting broad ridge, the traverse of which outdoor writer Chris Townsend refers to as "hillwalking at its finest", leads to the next Munro, at 1070m (3510ft).

From here, in poor visibility, the next section from the cairn to the bealach can be tricky. North-west from the second, lower summit, is a steep descent route east to the Bealach an Fhiodha. Its start is a couple of hundred metres south of Pt 993m.

From the bealach, a path takes a rising traverse to the ridge leading to Carn nan Gabhar. The ground is stony and the summit is not the trig point, but the large cairn some distance beyond. At 1121m (3678ft) it's the highest peak of the day.

Descending south-west takes you over Airgiod Bheinn ("the silver hill"), it's not a

Munro but a lovely final summit on a grand day out. Traversing rough moorland south-east takes you once again to the access track and what will feel like a long walk back to the start.

Approaching Carn Liath

RIGHT OF WAY

Nearby Glen Tilt played an important role in establishing the public right of access to Scotland's countryside.

On August 21, 1847, Edinburgh University botany professor James Balfour led a party of students through Glen Tilt en route to Blair Atholl.

The group, on a field trip, left Braemar that morning, travelling by carriage to upper Glen Tilt. Balfour was certain the route was a right of way but, as they neared the foot of the glen, they found their way barred by the Duke of Atholl's ghillies.

A three-hour stand-off ensued, with the Duke himself arriving to remonstrate with the party. He insisted they return to Braemar – hardly a realistic request. Eventually the professor and students leapt a dyke and made for Blair Atholl, pursued all the way by the Duke's men.

The so-called "Battle of Glen Tilt" led to a lengthy court battle that eventually saw the right of way through the glen recognised in law.

Did You Know?

Professor James Balfour, of Battle of Glen Tilt fame, was related to renowned geologist James Hutton. Hutton was Balfour's father's cousin and studied the geology of the glen in 1785.

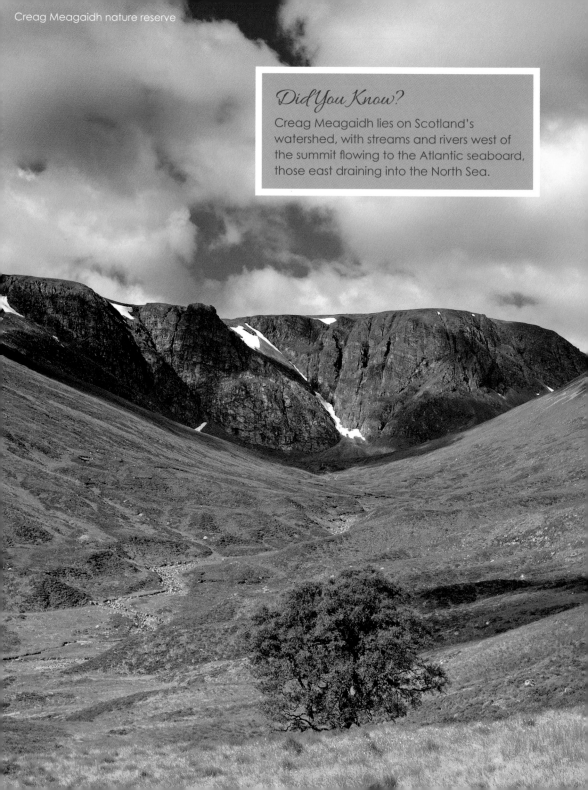

Creag Meagaidh nature reserve

15
Creag Meagaidh

A MASSIVE lump of a mountain that sits on the spine of Scotland, Creag Meagaidh is a highlight of any Munro round.

Just west of Loch Laggan, in Glen Spean, Creag Meagaidh is more a massif than a mountain – its vast plateau has four subsidiary tops, and, separated from the plateau by the glacial notch known as "The Window" are two more Munros, Stob Poite Coire Ardair and Carn Liath.

Munro-baggers tend to climb all three together, in a fine high-level walk of 21km (13.1 miles) and 1100m (3600ft) of ascent that will take about 8 hours.

To get a proper feel for this huge mountain, however, takes several visits. I've recommended it as a single, as the route, I think, gives a nice taste of the best of the mountain. It takes you first into the grand amphitheatre of Coire Ardair, then through The Window and, after the summit, along the rim of the cliffs that tower above the corrie, before finally descending easy slopes through vast patches of wonderfully aromatic bog myrtle. It's a superb day out.

The mountain can also be traversed but this means leaving a car, or arranging transport, at Moy or Aberarder, depending on where you start.

Coire Ardair is a famous climbing venue – attracting climbers from all over the

Pronunciation: *Craig Meggy*
Meaning: crag of the boggy place
Height: 1130m (3707ft); Rank: 29
OS Landranger Maps 34 & 42
Summit grid ref: NN418875 (cairn)

world. There's not much summer climbing – the cliffs are far too wet and vegetated – but as a winter venue they're second only to Ben Nevis.

The great cliffs of the corrie are some of the highest in the British Isles. Facing north-east, they get little sun and hold snow and ice late into spring. Most routes are long and in the higher grades – not for beginners. The mountain is also a notorious avalanche spot.

The extensive summit plateau is an undulating, rather featureless area – in foul weather navigation is difficult. Coming up from The Window, you reach an enormous, ancient cairn known as "Mad Meg's Cairn". It's often mistaken for the summit.

The origin of the cairn's name is lost in the mists of time. The outdoor writer and broadcaster Cameron McNeish cites a local legend that says it marks the grave of an 18th-century suicide. Denied a churchyard burial her family, the story goes, instead carried her on to the mountain.

NEAREST TOWN: Newtonmore is around 32km (19.9 miles) north-east. The vibrant Highland village has all amenities. Around 24km (14.9 miles) south-west is Spean Bridge, a smaller centre and home to the famous Commando Bar.

RECOMMENDED ROUTE

Start grid ref: NN482872
Distance: 16km (9.9 miles)
Ascent: 1080m (3543ft)
Time: 7hrs

THE ROUTE

There's ample parking in the National Nature Reserve car park, on the north side of the A86 at Aberarder. The reserve is well signposted.

From the car park, head down to the whitewashed former farm buildings that now house the reserve offices. There are public toilets here.

An excellent path leads through the gorgeous regenerating native woodland – the trees are mostly young and it'll be many decades before the land truly recovers from the overgrazing that blights so much of the Highlands.

A tiny cairn marks the start of a boggy path north to Carn Liath, for those planning a circuit of the three Munros.

Otherwise, keep following the track high on the north bank of the Allt Coire Ardair. As it curves round to the west, the mighty cliffs of Coire Ardair are revealed. It's an awesome sight. The closer you get,

94

the smaller you feel – I like to think a walk here is a useful lesson in objectivity, and a reminder of our place in the scheme of things . . .

On reaching Coire Lochan, head west for The Window – the notch is unmistakable. The Window is also where those climbing the two neighbouring Munros will end up.

From the bealach, it's a steep climb south on to the plateau – it's grassy and soft underfoot, making for pleasant walking.

Heading initially south, then south-west, you arrive at Mad Meg's Cairn – it's huge and many mistake it for the summit in poor visibility. The true summit is a few hundred metres west.

The route out cuts east across the plateau, then follows the rim of the great cliffs to Puist Coire Ardair. Again, take care in poor visibility. From that top, continue to Sron a' Choire, then bear east down easy slopes toward Aberarder. A bridge at NN475874 takes you over the Allt Coire Ardair.

Creag Meagaidh, winter

DOTTEREL AND BUNTING

Creag Meagaidh is a national nature reserve, cared for by Scottish National Heritage.

The upland site covers almost 4000 hectares (approx.10,000 acres) and is home to many rare mountain plants, like alpine speedwell, tufted saxifrage and woolly willow.

Bird life on the plateau includes the very rare dotterel, and the land above the 750m (2460ft) contour has been designated a Special Protection Area. Snow bunting also nest on the upper slopes.

The area, part of the Moy Estate, was purchased in 1985 by the old Nature Conservancy Council after the owners were denied permission to plant extensive conifer forestry.

The culling of deer has allowed native plants and woodland to regenerate naturally – there has been no planting on the reserve. Birch, willow and rowan abound.

Wetter ground is carpeted by a lush carpet of bog myrtle. Walking through it releases its wonderful scent – which makes up for the soaking your feet get.

Did You Know?

Scottish National Heritage have recorded 137 different species of bird in the Creag Meagaidh National Nature Reserve.

Nearing the summit of Meall Garbh

View from the summit of Meall Garbh

16
Meall Garbh

LYING hidden from easy view to the north of Loch Tay, Meall Garbh is very much the "forgotten" Munro of the Lawers group.

Its immediate neighbour, Meall Greigh, can be seen rising above the hamlet of Lawers from the road, while mighty Ben Lawers itself is much higher. Meall Garbh also lacks the rocky drama of the real star of this tight group of Munros, An Stuc.

However, Munro-baggers will, naturally enough, want to climb Meall Garbh simply by dint of its hallowed Munro status, but even the casual hillwalker has good reason to summit the peak – the views from the top are astonishing. It's the best viewpoint for rugged An Stuc – the summit of which is just 1km (0.6 miles) to the south-west and which is exactly the same height as Meall Garbh, but was only granted Munro status in the 1997 revision. The enormous bulk of Ben Lawers looms behind.

Beyond these mountains, to the west, the land is rumpled by layer after layer of hill. It's quite beautiful.

In good weather, a fine winter outing is to tackle Meall Garbh along with Meall Greigh. Terrain is generally easy going. I've snowshoed the round in well under six hours and it's the route I recommend here – snowshoes optional of course!

Another popular route is the circuit of

Pronunciation: *Me-yal Gar-av*
Meaning: rough rounded hill
Height: 1118m (3668ft); Rank: 36
OS Landranger Map 51
Summit grid ref: NN644436 (cairn)

the pretty Lochan nan Cat and includes An Stuc as a third Munro. The route up this hill from the bealach with Meall Garbh is a scramble on loose and, when wet, very slippy rock. Care is needed – and in winter it's a very challenging ascent.

If transport can be arranged, a traverse of these three Munros along with Ben Lawers and Beinn Ghlas is a marvellous day out – probably the best hillwalk in the area. Start with Meall Greigh and end at the National Trust for Scotland car park at the foot of Beinn Ghlas. It's roughly 18km (11.2 miles) with 1800m (5900ft) of ascent and you should allow up to 10 hours.

Meall Garbh

NEAREST TOWN: Killin lies about 13km (8 miles) south-west. There are plenty of places to eat and drink, a variety of shops, including an outdoor store and supermarket, plus accommodation from holiday parks to hotels. A visit to the preserved Moirlanich Longhouse gives a rare insight into 19th-century life.

RECOMMENDED ROUTE
Start grid ref: NN677395
Distance: 15.5km (9.6 miles)
Ascent: 1200m (3937ft)
Time: 6hrs

THE ROUTE

Cars can be left in the Lawers Hotel car park – so long as you buy some food or drink on your return. Seems a fair deal – certainly given the superb food and range of real ales I've always enjoyed there. I recommend the hot chocolate for drivers!

Head west along the A827 for a few hundred metres, to a bend where the horn carver's cottage sits. From here, a good path follows the Lawers Burn, initially on the right bank, but crossing over to the left, east bank, after about 2km (1.2 miles).

Continue on this path for around another 1km (0.6 miles) to where it merges with a vehicle track. This leads, in

THE HAUNTING OF LAWERS

Lawers was once a much larger settlement than the scattering of houses it consists of today.

It was home to a number of farmsteads, and the remains of the abandoned village can still be seen. They include homes, a church and a mill.

The village is reputed to be haunted by the Lady of Lawers. She lived in the area in the 17th century and was said to have the gift of prophecy. She was buried next to an ash tree in the churchyard. She'd earlier warned that anyone harming the tree would meet a bad end. In the 1870s, it was chopped down by local farmer John Campbell – who was later gored to death by his own bull. The man who helped him fell the tree went mad, and the horse that pulled the cart dropped down dead.

Other predictions apparently foretold the Clearances and the age of steamships and tourism.

a short distance, to a hydro dam. Cross the river beyond the dam, taking care, before heading north-north-west up grassy, steepening slopes. Keep left of the slight ravine as you trend round above craggier ground to join the ridge that will lead to Meall Garbh's summit.

From the summit, follow the ridge back to the bealach with Meall Greigh. From here, it's a case of following the broad crest of the ridge over the second Munro. Gradients are quite easy, and it's a pleasant walk. The summit is 1001m (3284ft) and has good views into the Glen Lyon hills.

Head south over Sron Mhor to eventually pick up the path of your inward route.

© STEVEN FALLON

Did You Know?

According to the Scottish Mountaineering Club, Beinn na Lap is the third most common hill on which walkers finish, or "compleat", their Munro round.

17

Beinn na Lap

REGARDED as one of the easiest Munros to climb, Beinn na Lap is, conversely, one of the most difficult to reach.

The only practical route to it is by train. You could also cycle in from Fersit in the north or Dalwhinnie in the north-east – but rail is the sensible option for those looking for a day out, rather than an expedition.

The foot of the hill is barely more than 1km (0.6 miles) from Corrour Station, on the West Highland Line.

The station lies at 408m (1339ft) above sea level and the hill itself is gently rounded, with generally easy slopes. It's not a tough day out… normally. In his book *Scotland*, outdoor writer Chris Townsend describes being forced to abandon a winter ascent of the hill in winds so strong he was unable to stand, while underfoot was rock-solid ice.

Beinn na Lap is also a very popular hill, as I discovered when I climbed it in June 2017, it being the final mountain I had to ascend to "compleat" the Munros.

There were 20-odd people in my party. On the hill that day were two other quite large, and unconnected, groups. I was stunned to discover they included two others also finishing the Munros that day.

We had a bit of a joint celebration at the summit, with champagne, whisky

> Pronunciation: *Ben nah Lap*
> Meaning: dappled hill
> Height: 935m (3068ft); Rank: 241
> OS Landranger Map 41
> Summit grid ref: NN376695 (cairn)

and cake consumed. I do not normally condone drinking in the hills – it can dangerously affect judgement and so on – but I do confess the rest of that day is a wee bit of a blur. Especially after some more celebratory beers back at Corrour Station, which houses a fantastic restaurant and bar with rooms.

I found out later from Dave Broadhead, clerk of lists at the Scottish Mountaineering Club, that Beinn na Lap is the third most popular Munro for people to finish on, behind Ben Hope and Ben More on Mull. And here was me thinking I was being original…

I suppose the fact it's a bit harder to reach means some might leave Beinn na Lap until last. My own reasons were that, being such an "easy" Munro, it meant people who weren't used to hillwalking could join me, while the romance of a train journey – particularly that of the stunning West Coast Line – added something extra special to the day.

NEAREST TOWN: Roybridge is 16km (9.9 miles) north-west and lies on the railway that takes you to Corrour – the stop for Beinn na Lap. It has plenty of accommodation and good options for food and drink.

RECOMMENDED ROUTE

Start grid ref: NN356664
Distance: 10km (6.2 miles)
Ascent: 560m (1837ft)
Time: 3.5hrs

THE ROUTE

From Corrour Station, a hard-core Land Rover track leads east to Loch Ossian.

It's a beautiful little loch, with tiny islands covered in native pine. On a small headland sits Loch Ossian Youth Hostel, one of the most remote – and basic – in Scotland. After being hooked up to a local hydro-electric scheme it does now boast hot showers!

After just over 1km (0.6 miles), turn left at a fork before – after a few hundred metres – leaving the track for a path that fords a stream and then climbs north up Beinn na Lap's broad, grassy slopes.

The views back to little Loch Ossian are very pretty.

The going is quite easy all the way to the wide ridge of Ceann Caol Beinn na Lap. The ridge runs just north of east and takes you gently to the summit.

Views from the summit cairn are quite wonderful – there's the vast expanse of Rannoch Moor, which can seem more water than land, bordered to the north and west by the great, soaring peaks of the West Highlands.

Easiest way back to the station is by the route of ascent.

Celebrating the "Munros Round"

Did You Know?

Inaccessible by public road, Corrour Rail Halt is the most remote station of the UK's mainline rail network. At 408m (1339ft) above sea level it's also the highest.

TRAINSPOTTING

If Corrour Station feels a bit familiar it's probably because it's something of a movie star.

The station featured in the Scottish cult classic *Trainspotting*, when characters Renton, Sick Boy and Spud, played by Ewan McGregor, Jonny Lee Miller and Ewen Bremner, are dragged to the Highlands to "experience" Scotland's great outdoors by Tommy, played by Kevin McKidd.

The mountain that features in the famous scene is a Corbett, Leum Uilleim, a short distance west of Beinn na Lap and the station.

Filming for the movie's sequel, *Trainspotting 2*, also took place at Corrour Station.

The rail line south of Corrour also starred in *Harry Potter and the Deathly Hallows Part 1*, in a scene in which Death Eaters stop the Hogwarts Express train before boarding it for inspection.

Corrour Station was built by the West Highland Railway and has operated since 1894. It also housed a Post Office, which closed in 1977.

The twin peaks of the Easains, Stob Coire Easain and Stob a' Choire Mheadhoin

© JOHN McSPORRAN

Did You Know?

In his book *Hamish's Mountain Walk*, mountaineer Hamish Brown refers to Stob Coire Easain and Stob a' Choire Mheadhoin as "This Yin" and "That Yin".

Road end at Fersit. Route to Stob Coire Easain is over Meall Cian Dearg on the right

18
Stob Coire Easain

ANOTHER Munro that comes with a twin, and I imagine everyone who climbs Stob Coire Easain will also climb its sister, Stob a' Choire Mheadhoin. Indeed, the pair are often collectively referred to simply as "the Easains".

The hills lie several kilometres south of the A86 and Roybridge on the edge of some truly wild country. The vast, empty-feeling Rannoch Moor is a short distance south.

The pair of mountains are similar in height – Stob Coire Easain at 1115m (3658ft) is just 10m (33ft) taller than Stob a' Choire Mheadhoin. The summits are only about 1km (0.6 miles) apart, separated by a high col at 960m (3150ft).

From particular viewpoints in the south they do indeed look like twin peaks – Stob Coire Easain is the finer of the pair, I feel. It's a more satisfying climb from the shared col – steeper, rougher with a couple of wee rocky steps.

The views from the top are quite magnificent – the Grey Corries, the Aonachs and the grandest of them all, Ben Nevis, are incredibly impressive looking west. South, Rannoch Moor appears endless.

The easiest approach to the hills is from Fersit – a tiny hamlet several kilometres down a scenic single-track road from the A86.

Pronunciation: *Stob Cor-ye Essan*
Meaning: peak of the corrie of the little waterfall
Height: 1115m (3658ft); Rank: 39
OS Landranger Map 41
Summit grid ref: NN308730 (cairn)

It lies just at the head of gloomy looking Loch Treig – a deep trench of a loch, like a land-locked fjord with the Easains forming a very steep western wall, the Munro of Stob Coire Sgriodain doing similar in the east.

The loch is a reservoir, dammed in 1929 and flooding the old settlements of Kinlochtreig and Creaguaineach, which occupied land at the southern end of the loch. At one time, they'd been the location of large cattle markets, sitting on important droving routes.

As part of the Lochaber hydro-electric scheme, the loch was linked to the aluminium smelter in Fort William by a 24km (14.9 mile) tunnel hacked through the mountains.

The loch has long been associated in folklore with malicious sprites like kelpies and water bulls. In 1933, divers working on the hydro project asked to be moved to other jobs after they claimed to have seen terrible creatures in underwater caverns.

Loch Treig below Stob Coire Easain and Stob a' Choire Mheadhoin

NEAREST TOWN: There is accommodation – from bunkhouses to hotels – around Roybridge, roughly 8.6km (5.3 miles) north-west. A further 5km (3.1 miles) further west is Spean Bridge, a village at the junction of the A82 and A86. It has a small selection of shops and a slightly wider range of places to eat and drink. There's plenty of accommodation options nearby, including the Spean Bridge Hotel. The iconic Commando Memorial lies 1.6km (1 mile) west of the village.

RECOMMENDED ROUTE
Start grid ref: NN349781
Distance: 17km (10.6 miles)
Ascent: 1170m (3839ft)
Time: 6hrs

The story was reported in *The Scotsman* newspaper on October 25 that year.

THE ROUTE

There's a large parking and turning area at the hamlet of Fersit, just north of Loch Treig.

The hamlet's reached by twisting, narrow single track that leads off the A86 near Tulloch Station – the turning is 7.5km (4.7 miles) east of Roy Bridge.

The 6km (3.7 mile) ridge that leads to the summit starts practically at the car park – it is quite boggy terrain though.

Better to stick on the vehicle track by the loch for about 1km (0.6 miles) beyond the dam. On reaching two turn-offs to the right, take the second. The going can be wet and muddy until after you gain the ridge, near a huge concrete survey pillar.

The way to Stob a' Choire Mheadhoin seems barred by Meall Cian Dearg, which rises impressively steeply ahead. In reality the scrambly path picks its way easily enough through any difficulties – indeed the drier underfoot conditions will be welcome.

Did You Know?

The Easains rise above Loch Treig, whose name translates, rather ominously, as "loch of death".

Beyond this, the ridge becomes broad and quite featureless. A couple of flatter sections and short pulls take you to the summit at 1105m (3625ft).

Stony slopes south-west take you to the col with Stob Coire Easain at 960m (3150ft) – the next Munro looks an impressive cone from here. The going's steep but never difficult, although the path is eroded in sections.

The easiest route of return is to retrace your steps, climbing over the first Munro once. An alternative is to descend north-west from the col into Coire Laire, gradually trending north-east to pick up a track along the river and back to the start. Having walked both, I found this route rougher and much longer. It's perhaps a good option in windy weather when an escape from the ridge would be more comfortable.

INVERLAIR LODGE

On the road to Fersit, and the start of this route, you pass Inverlair Lodge.

The old house was requisitioned by the Special Operations Executive during the Second World War.

It was used by the SOE to house "failed" British spies – people deemed too incompetent to serve, but whose training meant they knew too much to simply be allowed to return to either the regular forces or civilian life.

They lived in relative comfort but in what was effectively an open jail. The house is said to be the inspiration for the cult 1960s TV show *The Prisoner*, starring Patrick McGoohan.

One of the unfortunate residents was sent to Inverlair for being so "outstandingly ugly" it was impossible for him to be a successful spy. Declassified documents state: "He'd be recognised anywhere. Once seen, never forgotten. He had no teeth at all except two gold tusks and two incisors."

Meall nan Tarmachan from Ben Lawers

© JOHN McSPORRAN

The Tarmachan Ridge

19
Meall nan Tarmachan

JUST north of the picturesque Stirlingshire tourist town of Killin lies Meall nan Tarmachan.

It's the highest peak – and only Munro – of a snaking, sinuous group of hills that make up the Tarmachan Ridge, famously the narrowest mountain ridge in what was once Perthshire.

Meall nan Tarmachan can be climbed as a simple there-and-back Munro in a few hours from the National Trust for Scotland Ben Lawers car park – but to miss out the ridge is to forego one of the best hillwalks in Central Scotland. It's a spectacular day out.

The other peaks on the Tarmachan Ridge are Meall Garbh, Beinn nan Eachan and Creag na Caillich.

The best view of the hills is from Killin. They rise in a steep wall above the town, the gnarled rocky ridge making for a very impressive skyline.

The route to the Munro follows a decent path and is relatively simple – indeed, despite measuring a mighty 1044m (3425ft), the high start from the car park at about 450m (1476ft) makes Meall nan Tarmachan one of the easiest Munros.

That said, it took me a few attempts to climb it – including one in which I couldn't even make it to the car park, as the untreated, single-track road was buried in deep drifts. And the first time I actually

> Pronunciation: *Me-yal nun Tar-mach-an*; Meaning: hill of the ptarmigan
> Height: 1044m (3425ft); Rank: 89
> OS Landranger Map 51
> Summit grid ref: NN585390 (cairn)

summited the Munro, severe winds, blizzards and a complete lack of visibility meant just retracing the route to the car felt like an achievement. Attempting the ridge would have been plain daft.

In good conditions, the ridge is an exciting day out. It's also relatively short – making it a viable, if challenging, winter day out, providing you make it to the car park.

In summer, the clear path – worn by the passage of thousands of boots – makes the route choice obvious. The way is narrow in places – with some big drops and crags – but the scrambling is never difficult.

The hardest section is Grade 1 and is easily avoidable on a bypass path.

On the summit of Meall nan Tarmachan

Tarmachan Hills across Loch Tay

NEAREST TOWN: Killin lies about 7km (4.4 miles) south-west. There are plenty of places to eat and drink, a variety of shops, including an outdoor store and supermarket, plus accommodation from holiday parks to hotels. The Falls of Dochart Inn – an 18th-century blacksmith's forge – is a great spot for a pint.

RECOMMENDED ROUTE
Start grid ref: NN608377
Distance: 13km (8.1 miles)
Ascent: 750m (2461ft)
Time: 5hrs

THE ROUTE

A superb path leads from the track out of the Ben Lawers National Trust car park (charge). It leads to another vehicle track – walk straight across this.

Continue on the path up grassy slopes all the way to Meall nan Tarmachan's south-east top at 923m (3028ft).

The path then descends very slightly and leads over a flatter section before climbing steeply through crags and steeper ground to the summit. The views over to Ben Lawers are fine – but the best of the day awaits.

First head south, then south-west to a bealach with two lochans – it's then a steep, brief climb up rocky ground to the summit of Meall Garbh. The path leads to a wonderful grassy arête – the narrowest section of the ridge.

Winter on the climb up Meall nan Tarmachan

After the arête is a rocky descent – a Grade 1 scramble and the trickiest part of the route. There is a bypass path for those who don't fancy it.

Next top is Beinn nan Eachan – again a clear path leads to the next bealach. It's worthwhile climbing the final top – Creag na Caillich, a nice rocky wee peak. Easiest descent is to return to the bealach, before picking your way south-east down steep, grassy slopes into the Coire Fionn Lairige.

On reaching a disused quarry, turn left along the old access road. It's roughly 4km (2.5 miles) back to the start point.

The Tarmachan Hills

THE STONE AGE
The area around Meall nan Tarmachan has an amazingly rich history, with evidence of human occupation going back many thousands of years.

Some 600m (1968ft) up on Creag na Caillich, the most westerly of the Tarmachan Ridge's peaks, is the site of an ancient stone-axe production site.

It's a very rare site – one of just a handful known in the UK. The earliest evidence of quarrying for stone to make the axe heads dates to almost 3000 BC. It was the time of the Neolithic in Scotland – the "New Stone Age", and the time of the first farmers.

On the Edramucky Burn, on the slopes of nearby Ben Lawers, evidence of even earlier activity has been discovered.

Archaeologists have uncovered the site of a temporary campsite used by hunter-gatherers in the Mesolithic era – the "Middle Stone Age". Radiocarbon dating of burnt remains dates the site to an incredible 9000 years ago.

Meall na Teanga and Sron a' Choire Ghairbh over Loch Lochy

Did You Know?

The track from the start of the eastern route to the Cam Bhealach follows an old "coffin road", along which people from remote settlements would carry their dead to the graveyard at Kilfinnan.

Meall na Tanga from Geall Charn

20

Meall na Teanga

O N the north side of Loch Lochy, Meall na Teanga and its near neighbour, the Munro Sron a' Choire Ghairbh, rise steeply to dominate the area.

The hills are the highest along the length of the Great Glen – the area's only Munros – and are most often climbed together. Indeed, many simply refer to them as the Loch Lochy Munros.

There are two routes of ascent by which the hills are most commonly climbed. One is from the Forestry Commission car park just east of Loch Arkaig, near the Eas Chia-aig waterfalls.

The other is from Kilfinnan, near the head of Loch Lochy.

Having walked both routes, I'd recommend the former. The route from Loch Arkaig, follows Gleann Cia-aig, and then a very boggy, rough and trackless section. It makes for slow progress and can be quite tiring – the high bealach between the Munros never seems to get any closer!

It is, however, among satisfyingly remote and wild-feeling country. A good route if you want to avoid the crowds. The return from Meall na Teanga takes you over the Munro's southern top, Meall Coire Lochain – an ascent that takes you along a lovely narrow ridge with some very minor scrambling.

> Pronunciation: *Me-yal na Chen-ga*
> Meaning: hill of the tongue
> Height: 918m (3012ft); Rank: 275
> OS Landranger Map 34
> Summit grid ref: NN220925 (cairn)

The Kilfinnan route initially follows forestry roads along what is now the Great Glen Way and an excellent path up to the bealach. It makes for much easier and faster going – but the conifer plantations early on in the walk, some of which have been cleared, aren't as pretty as the wild lands of the route from the west. It's certainly a quicker and simpler way to the hill – but lacks much of the character of the former.

The views from Meall na Teanga are fantastic – Ben Nevis to the south looks grand, while the narrow ridge of the descent route lures you on.

The high bealach between Sron a' Choire Ghairbh and Meall na Teanga

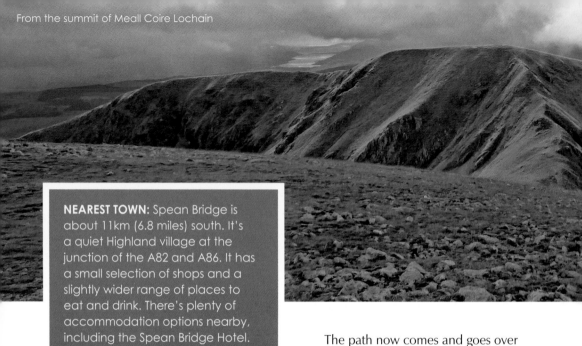

NEAREST TOWN: Spean Bridge is about 11km (6.8 miles) south. It's a quiet Highland village at the junction of the A82 and A86. It has a small selection of shops and a slightly wider range of places to eat and drink. There's plenty of accommodation options nearby, including the Spean Bridge Hotel. The iconic Commando Memorial lies 1.6km (1 mile) west of the village. From Spean Bridge the large town of Fort William is 15km (9.3 miles) south-west.

RECOMMENDED ROUTE
Start grid ref: NN177889
Distance: 21km (13 miles)
Ascent: 1630m (5348ft)
Time: 8hrs

THE ROUTE

There's a large forestry car park off the single-track B8005 road, near the east end of Loch Arkaig, for the Eas Chia-aig waterfalls.

From here, a path zig-zags north to a rough forest/hydro road. This runs up Gleann Cia-aig for several kilometres. A path continues the route to a footbridge over which you cross the Abhainn Chia-aig.

The path now comes and goes over what can be very boggy, tussocky terrain. Keep trending east toward the Cam Bhealach. Eventually another track is met, which carries you to the col.

Turn left here and follow a zig-zag path up the steep, grassy southern flank of Sron a' Choire Ghairbh. When the path ends, it's an easy walk to gain the ridge. Gentle slopes take you north-west for a few hundred metres to the summit at 937m (3074ft). Return to the bealach.

Climb south, initially over quite eroded ground, then traverse the hillside to reach the col between Meall Dubh and Meall na Teanga. The path is obvious. From here it's a steep pull south up to the summit ridge – passing first a small cairn, before reaching the larger summit cairn after a few hundred metres more.

Now lies perhaps the best part of the day – the narrow ridge walk over Meall

Choire Chairbh

Did You Know?

It's not just Loch Ness that has a monster – a large serpentine-like creature is said to inhabit Loch Lochy. She's known locally as "Lizzie".

Coire Lochain. Head south-west to the col, then climb the rocky ridge. It gets increasingly steep before ending at a large, gently sloping plateau.

Head west for perhaps 1.5km (0.9 miles) then descend the grassy, easy slopes north of the Allt a' Chlamhan. Aim to pick up your original inward path just north of the forest. Once reached, simply follow it back to the car.

Route of the descent

THE CALEDONIAN CANAL

Meall na Teanga rises above Loch Lochy, which is linked to Loch Oich and Loch Ness in turn to form the Caledonian Canal.

The canal provides a navigable route for boats between the Irish Sea and the North Sea, from Corpach, near Fort William, in the west, to Inverness.

The route meant cargo and fishing boats could avoid the longer – and very treacherous – journey around the storm-lashed north-west of Scotland.

The idea for the canal dates from the 19th century. Engineer James Watt – of steam-engine fame – was commissioned in 1773 to examine the feasibility of the route.

Later, Thomas Telford looked at the issue. He began construction of the canal in 1803, though it didn't open until 1822 – 12 years later than expected.

The entire route is 97km (60.3 miles) long, including the lochs. The constructed parts of the canal are 35km (21.7 miles) long. It includes 29 locks – eight on the famous Neptune's Staircase at Corpach.

The Mamores from Aonach Eagach

WESTERN
HIGHLANDS

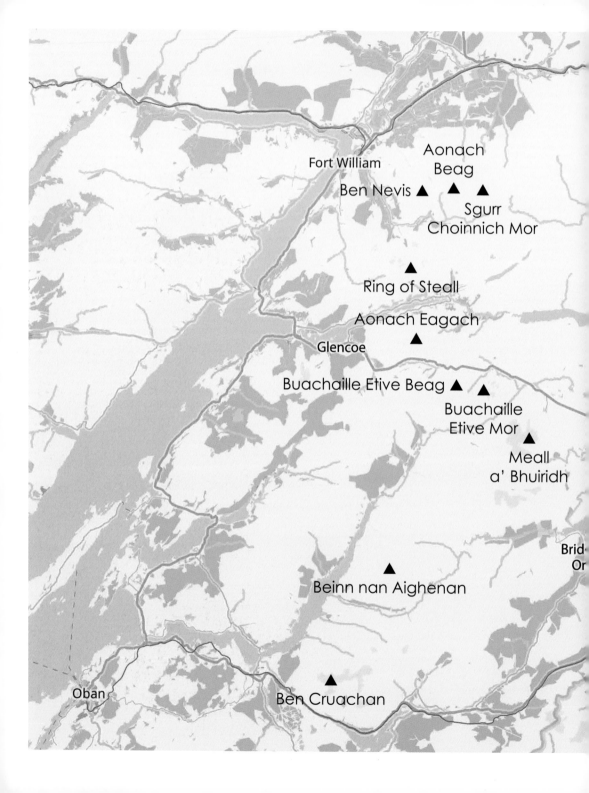

Rannoch

Ben Cruachan summit

Did You Know?

Loch Awe is the longest freshwater loch in Scotland, measuring 41km (25.5 miles). It's the third-largest in terms of surface area, behind Loch Lomond and Loch Ness.

Ben Cruachan from Beinn Lora

21
Ben Cruachan

THE highest of a popular group of four Munros and a Corbett near Dalmally, Ben Cruachan is one of Scotland's most famous mountains.

It's an enormous hill, the highest for miles. It dominates its neighbours and is prominent in views from many other distant hills in the Central and Western Highlands.

Ben Cruachan is quite the perfect mountain, with four ridges rising from each point of the compass, culminating in a sharp, pleasingly pointed peak that towers over sinuous Loch Awe.

It can be climbed as a single hill, or in combination with its neighbours – a long traverse of all the Munros, with a high-level camp, is one of the finest mountain outings in the Highlands.

A much shorter outing, a wonderful horseshoe route circling Cruachan Reservoir and taking a second Munro, Stob Daimh, reveals much of the character of the mountain. It traverses grassy slopes, a band of massive boulders at the summit, and involves very minor scrambling and a lovely ridge walk. It's not huge in terms of distance, but involves much up and down and is a fairly testing day out.

On clear days the summit views out over the coast to the western islands, Mull particularly prominent, are spectacular.

Pronunciation: *Ben Croo-ach-an*
Meaning: heaped hill
Height: 1126m (3694ft); Rank: 31
OS Landranger Map 50
Summit grid ref: NN069304 (cairn & ruined trig point)

To the north, the ground drops away dramatically into great, scooped corries. The land below looks remote and wild. Beyond lie the tangled ridges and rumpled peaks of Glen Etive and Glen Coe.

It's always a busy hill but big enough to rarely feel crowded. The Cruachan Horseshoe is a marvellous round on the longer days of late winter, when the snow lies hard and thick. On those rare days, with a flawless, deep-blue sky, snow crunching under crampons and surrounded by the enormous hills that encircle the reservoir, creating an amphitheatre, the circuit feels like a proper mountain expedition.

Ben Cruachan from the Cruachan dam

Loch Etive from Ben Cruachan

NEAREST TOWN: Oban is roughly 24km (14.9 miles) west. It's one of the principal towns of the West Highlands. It's a port town, known as the "Gateway to the Hebrides" and has full accommodation options and a wealth of food, drink and leisure amenities.

RECOMMENDED ROUTE
Start grid ref: NN080267
Distance: 13km (8.1 miles)
Ascent: 1400m (4593ft)
Time: 8hrs

THE ROUTE

This is the classic Cruachan Horseshoe, starting at the Falls of Cruachan Railway Station. There's very limited parking in a rough layby at the station. If it's full, the nearest proper layby is some 700m (0.4 miles) west on the A85.

Head beneath the railway via an underpass – mind your head – then follow a clear track up through some quite dense but lovely woods full of native trees, especially birch.

Once out of the woodland, you will soon reach the power-station dam, which you climb by way of an iron ladder. On top of the dam, turn left then follow a surfaced track to the head of the loch. A small cairn indicates where you bear west, then north-west, to the bealach north of Meall Cuanail.

From here it's around 0.5km (0.3 miles) to Ben Cruachan's summit on increasingly steep and very rocky ground.

The route – initially north-west then west – along a winding rocky ridge, is clear. There is a slabby section, which presents some very simple scrambling. It can be bypassed on the right by a quite hefty descent then re-ascent if need be.

Once past the summit of Drochaid Ghlas, it's a fairly gentle pull up to Stob Daimh, the day's second Munro.

Head south and follow the ridge over the minor summit of Stob Garbh. Then

Ben Cruachan

continue almost to the bealach with the Corbett of Beinn a' Bhuiridh before heading east downhill toward the reservoir. Stick to the right bank of the burn. You'll pick up a path that takes you back to the dam, where you return to the start along the woodland path.

Loch Awe

THE HOLLOW MOUNTAIN

Ben Cruachan is also known as the "Hollow Mountain" as, 1km (0.6 miles) below the surface, it contains a vast cavern housing a power station.

Constructed between 1959 and 1965, Cruachan Power Station is truly one of the wonders of the Highlands. It's a magnificent feat of engineering – the gargantuan turbine hall is big enough to swallow the entire nave of Glasgow Cathedral.

It's a pumped-storage hydro-electric power station. Water is transported by pump from Loch Awe to the dammed reservoir. Here it is stored until the National Grid demands extra electrical capacity – for example, at the end of television programmes when millions of kettles can be switched on – when it's discharged to provide power.

Although hidden from sight, visitors get the chance to see this engineering marvel thanks to tours organised by owners Scottish Power. It's well worth a visit.

Stob Dearg (Buachaille Etive Mor)

Did You Know?

Glen Etive features in the 2012 James Bond film *Skyfall*, starring Daniel Craig, resulting in huge numbers of tourists visiting the once lonely glen.

22

Stob Dearg (Buachaille Etive Mor)

THE highest of four summits – two of them Munros – that make up the Buachaille Etive Mor, Stob Dearg is probably Scotland's most photographed peak.

Buachaille Etive Mor – the Great Herdsman of Etive, or simply "The Bookle" to generations of hill-goers, stands sentinel over the entrances to both Glen Etive and Glen Coe.

The iconic image of what is arguably Scotland's most famous mountain is of a formidable pyramid of rock, riven by gullies, craggy broken ridges and soaring cliff faces, well seen on the approach from the east across the watery expanse of Rannoch Moor. This is Stob Dearg.

From this angle, the prospect of an ascent will thrill some and intimidate others – and to be told you can simply walk to the top of this peak will initially seem absurd. But, on the hill's north side, the Coire na Tulaich offers a route that allows you to do just that – occasionally on steep, loose scree, but a relatively simple walk nonetheless.

Even the great craggy face of the Rannoch Wall offers a non-technical – but still serious – route for competent scramblers with a head for heights, Curved Ridge. Climbers, meanwhile, are spoilt for choice, with a plethora of routes of all

Pronunciation: *Stob Ger-ag (Boo-akle Etiv More)*; Meaning: red peak (Great Herdsman of Etive)
Height: 1021m (3350ft); Rank: 110
OS Landranger Map 41
Summit grid ref: NN222542 (small cairn)

grades. In winter, these multi-pitch routes offer an alpine-like experience, out of all proportion to the mountain's modest height.

However you get to the top, what awaits is an incredible vista from the airy summit – looking east, it's a sheer drop to the floor of Rannoch Moor. It feels like you're floating. West, the narrow ridge twists and turns and rises and falls on its way to Stob na Broige, the Buachaille's second Munro.

Buachaille Etive Mor has a special place in the history of the development of climbing in Scotland. The first rock climb here was by the great mountaineering pioneer Norman Collie in 1894.

Following decades saw new routes established by legendary climbers like William W. Naismith, Harold Raeburn and W. H. Murray – whose marvellous books, *Undiscovered Scotland* and *Mountaineering in Scotland,* give exciting accounts of

NEAREST TOWN: Glencoe is about 13km (8.1 miles) west. Although a small village it has great facilities. Accommodation options include hotels, B&Bs, caravan and campsites, and a youth hostel. There are shops, a petrol station and excellent places to eat and drink.

RECOMMENDED ROUTE
Start grid ref: NN221563
Distance: 13.5km (8.4 miles)
Ascent: 1150m (3373ft)
Time: 7hrs

climbs on the mountain from the 1930s onwards.

The hill's cultural significance, history, wonderful aesthetics and sheer mountaineering versatility make it one of my favourites. I've walked up it and strolled along the fantastic ridge that links all four peaks, I've scrambled on the superb rock with its big, deep holds and climbed thrillingly exposed routes on Rannoch Wall. It's a mountain I return to time and again, in all seasons, and could never tire of.

THE ROUTE
The above figures are for the superb ridge walk along the spine of Buachaille Etive

Mor – taking in both Munros, Stob Dearg and Stob na Broige.

However, I also recommend an ascent via Curved Ridge for competent scramblers – it has to be the most fun way up the hill for non-technical climbers.

Both routes start just off the A82 at Altnafeadh, where there is ample parking. Walk past the Lagangarbh Hut and, for the walking route, follow the excellent path right – it ascends into Coire na Tulaich. It's steep in places and winds its way through boulders and scree. Here and there are simple rocky steps that require some basic scrambling.

The path deteriorates as the terrain steepens below the corrie rim – the last stretch zig-zags up loose scree and eroded slopes and requires care.

In winter, considerable cornices can build here. The bowl of the corrie is a notorious avalanche "terrain trap" and many have died.

Above the corrie, Stob Dearg's dramatic summit lies to the left, the route marked by cairns. From there, retrace your steps back to the head of the corrie, before continuing along the well-defined ridge over Stob na Doire, Stob Coire Altruim and, finally, the Munro of Stob na Broige. The views along Glen Etive are spectacular.

Best descent is to return over Stob Coire Altruim. Just before the bealach, a rough path leads north to the Lairig Gartain, which will take you back to the A82, about 1km (0.6 mile) west of Altnafeadh.

One of the hardest parts of Curved Ridge is finding the start, especially in clag. Head left after Lagangarbh. A good path winds on to the north-east face, coming to an end at a tiny cairn. From there, a rising traverse – right initially, but then zig-zagging – will take you to the start of the ridge.

It curves up the mountain a short distance across a gully from, and on the left of, the mighty Rannoch Wall.

It's a stiff Grade 2/3 scramble. Holds are excellent and the sense of exposure thrilling. The 240m (787ft) route ends at Crowberry Tower, which can be bypassed on the left. The summit is easily gained on steep ground.

Climbing on the Rannoch Wall

CLEVER CROWS

Everyone knows crows are clever, but those on Stob Dearg appear smarter than most . . .

Climbers tackling routes on the Rannoch Wall often leave packs at the foot of the cliff, picking them up later on descent via Curved Ridge.

A few years ago, some complained their lunches and snacks had been stolen from their packs. Hungry after their exertions, the climbers were understandably miffed.

Complaints of food thefts persisted and became something of a mystery – until the corvid culprits were caught in the act.

Somehow – perhaps by observing what humans did – the birds figured out not only that the packs contained food, but how to access it by unfastening clips, loosening toggles, opening plastic containers and then munching the sandwiches.

Buachaille Etive Mor

Lagangarbh Hut at Buachaille Etive Beag

23

Stob Coire Raineach (Buachaille Etive Beag)

THE summit of Stob Coire Raineach is the smaller of two Munros on mighty Buachaille Etive Mor's little brother – Buachaille Etive Beag, or the "Wee Bookle".

The mountain runs parallel with its larger neighbour, and there are similarities between the two from certain angles on the A82.

From down Glen Etive's single-track road, however, the mountains look like twins – the wee Buachaille's Munro of Stob Dubh mirroring its counterpart on the big Buachaille, Stob na Broige. They form the incredibly steep, even sides to a perfect U-shaped glaciated valley, through which runs the Lairig Gartain.

Stob Coire Raineach is the summit lying closest to the A82. As well as being smaller than its neighbour, it lacks the drama and grandeur, and ascents are nowhere near as tough. Although, it is a rocky little peak and there are a couple of good scrambling routes up its nose.

Like all the Munros in Glencoe, it's an incredibly popular hill. Most often, it's climbed from the large car park across from the massive "beehive" cairn just off the main road. From there, it's a short haul of about 1km (0.6 miles) up the Lairig Eilde before a sharp climb south-east to the bealach, from where both summits can be picked off in turn.

> Pronunciation: *Stob Coy-er Ran-yach (Boo-akle Etiv Beg)*
> Meaning: peak of the bracken-filled corrie (Little Shepherd of Etive)
> Height: 925m (3035ft); Rank 263
> OS Landranger Map 41
> Summit grid ref: NN191548 (cairn)

Tackling it from the Glen Etive side, however, gives, I think, a much more pleasing ascent – even if it does mean starting a couple of hundred metres lower down. It's a very steep pull up Stob Dubh, but then you have a marvellous ridge walk to Stob Coire Raineach. The summit of this second Munro is a superb viewpoint for the serrated ridge of the infamous Aonach Eagach across Glen Coe, its jagged pinnacles cut into the skyline like the teeth of a saw.

Buachaille Etive Beag and the Lairig Gartain

NEAREST TOWN: Glencoe is about 11km (6.8 miles) west. Although a small village it has great facilities. Accommodation options include hotels, B&Bs, caravan and campsites and a youth hostel. There are shops, a petrol station and excellent places to eat and drink.

RECOMMENDED ROUTE
Start grid ref: NN169513
Distance: 8km (5 miles)
Ascent: 1100m (3609ft)
Time: 5.5hrs

THE ROUTE

I think most walkers prefer a circuit or a looped route, rather than an out-and-back. Somehow it's much more pleasing if you can avoid retracing your steps.

This route gives – pretty much – a loop, a fine ridge walk and two Munros, all in about five hours, give or take.

Start from Dalness, on the single-track road that runs down Glen Etive. There's a long, rough layby with enough room for several vehicles.

Cross the road and follow an excellent track on to the flank of Stob Dubh. A worn path takes you up the grassy south-west ridge. The going's steep, the climb unrelenting. The final section is very rocky but presents no difficulties.

The views south from the first summit are truly spectacular – Loch Etive, surely one of Scotland's most stunning, draws the eye to the coast. On clear days Mull and the Paps of Jura are clearly seen.

From here, the Munro summit is a short distance.

A wonderful narrow ridge leads to a point at 902m, and the bealach is easily gained on steeper ground.

Ahead is the rocky, stubby summit of Stob Coire Raineach. It's another steep ascent – and over very rough terrain – but it's short. A messy network of paths winds upwards to the summit – it's just a case of picking your line.

The summit is another fine viewpoint. To the east, Buachaille Etive Mor looks close enough to touch – walkers can be picked out on the summits and ridges. North-west is the dramatic Aonach Eagach, and beyond that Ben Nevis like a glowering titan looming over all.

From here, return with care on the rocky paths to the bealach. Descend south-east on steep grass to pick up the Lairig Gartain and head back to Dalness.

Did You Know?

The walk out on this route follows the Lairig Gartain. Lairig simply means "hill pass" in Gaelic.

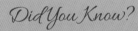
Buachaille Etive Beag

THE RIVER ETIVE

Through beautiful Glen Etive runs a short river of the same name.

It might just be 18km (11.2 miles) long but the River Etive is considered by kayakers to be one of the best in Scotland.

The section from the road bridge to Dalness in particular is regarded as a classic white-water run.

This 5km (3 mile) section consists of Grade 3 and 4 rapids, falls and plunge pools.

As well as walkers and kayakers, the glen is also incredibly popular with wild campers – in summer there can be scores of tents lining the roadside and grassy banks of the lower reaches of the river.

While the vast majority of visitors treat the environment with the appropriate care and respect, not all are so considerate. Sadly, in recent years – particularly after holiday weekends – considerable amounts of rubbish can be left behind, including abandoned tents and sleeping bags.

Did You Know?

It was in the Clachaig Inn, at the western end of Aonach Eagach, that Glencoe Mountain Rescue was formed in 1962 following a meeting chaired by famous climber Hamish MacInnes.

Aonach Eagach from Loch Achtriochtan

24
Meall Dearg (Aonach Eagach)

ONE of two Munros and four summits on the infamous Aonach Eagach, Meall Dearg offers one of the most thrilling ascents for hillwalkers in Scotland.

The Aonach Eagach is the sawtoothed ridge that bites savagely into the sky atop the massive wall of rock guarding the northern side of Glen Coe.

Meall Dearg sits at the heart of the ridge. The most common way of reaching it is from the east, after some exciting, exposed and challenging scrambling. Continuing west after the peak presents further scrambling – only this time more exciting, more exposed and more challenging. It's one of the finest mountain outings in all Scotland, certainly on the mainland.

Meall Dearg can also be climbed from the north, a route devoid of any scrambling difficulties – but where's the fun in that? It was via that route, however, that the first person to "compleat" the Munros, the Reverend A. E. Robertson, climbed what was the final hill of his round in 1901. Famously, on reaching the summit, the reverend kissed first the cairn and then his wife.

Much has been written of how difficult and terrifying the traverse of the Aonach Eagach is. It's a subjective thing and personally, I think the hype's a bit

Pronunciation: *Me-yal Ger-ag (E-noch Ee-gach)*
Meaning: red hill (notched ridge)
Height: 953m (3127ft); Rank: 212
OS Landranger Map 41
Summit grid ref: NN161584 (cairn)

overdone. It's a solid Grade 2 scramble, with excellent holds – it's like the rock was made for climbing – and in good conditions, competent, experienced scramblers will have a wonderful day.

Equally, I've seen those who dislike heights reduced to trembling wrecks – which begs the question, *if you don't like scrambling or heights, why would you put yourself through that?*

What makes Aonach Eagach a serious proposition is the exposure and commitment it demands. On the scrambling sections, there is no safe means of bypass or escape – you either go forward or back.

There are considerable drops and sections where mistakes would be costly – indeed, there have been fatalities over the years. Some parties will use ropes, probably more to inspire confidence than out of any real need.

In poor weather, with wet rock and anything above a stiff breeze, the traverse isn't so much fun and is best avoided.

Loch Leven from Sgorr nam Fiannaidh

NEAREST TOWN: Glencoe is about 8km (5 miles) west. Although a small village it has great facilities. Accommodation options include hotels, B&Bs, caravan and campsites and a youth hostel. Places to eat and drink include the Clachaig Inn, near the end of this route.

RECOMMENDED ROUTE
Start grid ref: NN174567
Distance: 9 km (5.6 miles)
Ascent: 1200m (3937ft)
Time: 6hrs

I've climbed it many times, in a variety of conditions. In winter it's a graded route (2/3) and depending on conditions can be a marvellous alpine-style ascent or a treacherous nightmare. My toughest traverse of the route was one February, when several inches of heavy, wet, fresh snow lay on iced-up rock. I love this route – but I can't honestly say that was a fun day.

THE ROUTE

This could be the easiest route description ever – climb to the ridge and follow it.

There's really nowhere else to go!

Most people traverse east to west – perhaps one of the reasons being that this saves 150m (492ft) of ascent. There's parking for several vehicles on the north side of the A82 a few hundred metres west of Allt-na-reigh. If this is full – and in good weather, unless you're very early, it likely will be – then there's a much larger car park a couple of hundred metres west on the opposite side of the road. It's an idea to leave a second car where you'll descend from the ridge, between the Clachaig Inn and Glencoe village. Otherwise it's a long 7km (4.4 mile) walk back to start. Hitching's an option but not everyone will stop for a bunch of smelly climbers.

A clear path – well maintained in sections – leads directly and steeply to Am Bodach, the ridge's most easterly summit. Beyond, you must down-climb to reach

The Pass of Glencoe from Am Bodach

the ridge proper. It's a drop of about 20m (66ft) – it's the route's first challenge and a taste of what the rest of the day will bring. Some parties will rope-up here, and it can appear a bit intimidating at first, but all the holds are there. It's best taken facing in.

The ridge, narrow in places and with minor scrambling in others, takes you to the central peak, the Munro Meall Dearg. The twisting, spire-filled ridge looks incredible from here – and it's now the real fun begins!

The Grade 2 scrambling isn't difficult – but it is exposed in places and feels serious, especially over the "Crazy Pinnacles" – towers of rock that must be traversed. Best advice is stick to the crest of the ridge and take everything head-on – it's easier than it looks.

All too soon the excitement is over and there's a long gradual pull to Sgorr nam Fiannaidh, another Munro.

By far the easiest descent is to continue along the ridge, before descending north-west to the bealach with Sgorr na Ciche (the Pap of Glencoe). A clear path, muddy and eroded in places, leads down to the road.

W. H. MURRAY

Renowned climber W. H. Murray is arguably the greatest mountain writer Scotland has produced. Two of his books, *Mountaineering in Scotland* and *Undiscovered Scotland* are regarded as classics of the mountaineering genre.

The books document many thrilling climbs and the development of the activity in Scotland from the 1930s to the 1950s. The first was written while Murray was a prisoner of the Germans during the Second World War.

The second book contains an incredible account of a traverse of the Aonach Eagach with his friend, Donald McIntyre, in February 1947. Wearing high-altitude flying suits, the pair arrived at the summit of Am Bodach, at the eastern end of the ridge, at 1.30a.m.

Under a bright moon, and in full winter conditions, they traversed the ridge, then reversed their route back along the ridge, arriving once again at the eastern end of the Aonach Eagach before daybreak.

Aonach Eagach

The summit of Ben Nevis

The summit of Ben Nevis from the top of the ledge route

Did You Know?

In 1911 Henry Alexander, the son of Scotland's first Ford dealer, drove a Model T car up and down Ben Nevis as a publicity stunt for the motoring firm.

25
Ben Nevis

THE Venomous Mountain, or the Hill of Heaven – two possible translations for the name Ben Nevis. Having climbed and walked many times on "the Ben" – the UK's highest mountain – I reckon both names apply.

The confusion is because the name's been so corrupted from the original Gaelic. It first appears as "Neevush" in the 1530s, then "Novesh" in 1595, not being written as "Nevis" until 1640.

Most commonly, the name's believed to come from the Gaelic "nibheis" – "venomous" or "evil". It probably refers to the horrendous weather that frequently engulfs the mountain.

The great naturalist Seton Gordon wrote that a popular traditional name for the mountain was "the Hill of Heaven". "Nevis" could be some corruption of the Gaelic "nèamhaidh" (heavenly).

Ben Nevis is also one of the most popular hills in Scotland, with an estimated 100,000 reaching the summit each year.

The vast majority walk there via the "Mountain Track", the name officially given in 2004 to the route popularly known as the "Tourist Path" after it was decided the old name probably encouraged too many ill-equipped summit attempts. By any route, Ben Nevis is a serious day out – the

Pronunciation: *Ben Nev-is*
Meaning: possibly venomous mountain, or Hill of Heaven
Height: 1345m (4413ft); Rank 1
OS Landranger Map 41
Summit grid ref: NN166712 (large cairn and trig point)

weather even in midsummer can be very cold, wet and windy.

I've always thought it's a shame the most popular route of ascent is also the least inspiring – the Mountain Track is a bit of a dull four-hour trudge. With scores – sometime hundreds – of other walkers on the route, it's also a very busy trudge.

Hidden from their view is the north face of the Ben – a dramatic arena of soaring cliffs, riven by great gullies and bolstered by towering rocky ridges. It's a sight that can be thrilling and terrifying in equal parts, and on an awesome scale that is befitting of our biggest mountain.

The north face is a world-famous rock- and ice-climbing venue. Many of the UK's greatest climbers cut their teeth here, and there are routes of all grades.

The summit consists of a large plateau, often snow-covered deep into summer. Cairns litter the area, and there's even a war memorial near the summit cairn.

NEAREST TOWN: Fort William is 6km (3.7 miles) north-west. Scotland's "Outdoor Capital", the large Highland town is home to 11,000 people and is well served by buses and trains. It has supermarkets, gear shops and lots of food, drink and accommodation options.

RECOMMENDED ROUTE
Start grid ref: NN144763
Distance: 18km (11.2 miles)
Ascent: 1500m (4921ft)
Time: 9hrs

On top of the observatory ruins sits a small emergency shelter – a welcome, if rather uncomfortable, refuge for those caught out by the ferocious conditions that can lash the summit year-round.

THE ROUTE
One of the best ways up "the Ben", as it's affectionately known, for non-climbers is via the Carn Mor Dearg arête.

It's a serious day out for experienced walkers who are happy with a bit of scrambling. It takes in the neighbouring Munro of Carn Mor Dearg (1220m;

4003ft), and leaves the Mountain Track for the descent.

You can start at the usual visitor-centre car park, cutting down to before the CIC Hut from the halfway lochan, but I think it's best to start from the north-face car park, near Torlundy. It's less overall ascent for the day – and it is also a bit quieter than the so-called "tourist route". I'm not anti-social . . . but that way is really crowded!

The track from the car park leads to a path signposted for the Allt a' Mhuilinn, reaching the river after about 2km (1.2 miles).

After walking beside the river for about 1km (0.6 miles), a rough path leads left up the broad ridge of Carn Mor Dearg. It's an easy walk to the ridge proper, which you join at Carn Dearg Meadhonach. From here, Carn Mor Dearg is a graceful cone. It's the ninth-highest Munro but is utterly dwarfed by the epic scale of the Ben.

The sweeping line of the arête draws

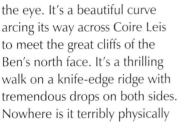

the eye. It's a beautiful curve arcing its way across Coire Leis to meet the great cliffs of the Ben's north face. It's a thrilling walk on a knife-edge ridge with tremendous drops on both sides.

Nowhere is it terribly physically demanding however.

Where the arête meets the Ben, a faint path winds through and over the enormous boulders that climb steeply toward the summit.

In poor weather, careful navigation is critical to safely descend from the plateau. Great cliffs await the unwary. Even into summer, they can be hidden beneath fragile cornices. Five Finger Gully is notorious for this, and there have been many fatalities over the years.

From the trig point, follow a compass bearing of 231 degrees for 150m (492ft), then a bearing of 282 degrees to the start of the zig-zags of the Mountain Track. Remember to add magnetic variation to these bearings – which should be listed on an up-to-date map.

The Track leads to the halfway lochan. From the head of the loch, head north-east over trackless ground to the Allt a' Mhuilinn and the path back out.

THE OBSERVATORY

The remains of a building can be seen on the summit of Ben Nevis. The ruin was once a weather observatory built by the Scottish Meteorological Society.

It operated continuously from 1883 until 1904 – the data collected remains the most complete meteorological data set from any UK summit.

The stone-built building was linked to Fort William by telegraph, and from 1897 by telephone. A spare room in the observatory – and later a four-room wooden shack – was known as the "Temperance Hotel", in which travellers could pay to spend the night. Refreshments and food were also served. The "hotel" continued to operate until 1916.

Before the observatory was built, meteorologist Clement Wragge climbed the mountain every day from mid June to mid October of 1881 to make observations – a feat he repeated the following year.

The path constructed up the mountain for the observatory, the Pony Track, is that used by tens of thousands of visitors today.

Carn Mor Dearg Arête and the Mamores

Glen Nevis from Ben Nevis

Meall an t-Suidhe from Ben Nevis (Half Way Lochan)

Ben Nevis, mountain track

Sgurr a' Mhaim and the Devil's Ridge

Did You Know?

With a single drop of 120m (394ft), Steall Falls are the second highest in the UK, behind Sutherland's Eas a' Chual Aluinn at 200m (656ft).

Mullach nan Coirean and Stob Ban

26
Sgurr a' Mhaim (Ring of Steall)

A MASSIVE lump of a mountain that rises sheer from the valley floor to form the southern wall of Glen Nevis, Sgurr a' Mhaim dominates the western view of the Mamores when approached from Fort William.

It can be climbed as a single Munro from Polldubh – either as a there-and-back, or more preferably as a circuit, taking in the wonderful "Devil's Ridge" arête that links the hill to the main Mamores ridge.

It's not how I'd recommend climbing the hill though. The ascent is unrelentingly steep. Sure, it gets you there quick – but I'd struggle to describe it as pleasant.

And as a single, even including the Devil's Ridge, you're missing out on one of the finest mountain walks in all Scotland – a true classic, the Ring of Steall.

There are 10 Munros on the Mamores ridge. They can all be done in a day – a very long, tiring but incredibly rewarding day. I walked it a couple of years ago with Iain Cameron, the man who records Scotland's snow patches. It was a 40km (25 mile) route with around 3000m (9843ft) of ascent and took 12 hours.

Most sensible people will opt to break the ridge into chunks, and the hills are nicely grouped for this. From the east, they neatly fall into sets of four, four and two

Pronunciation: *S-goo-r a Vime*
Meaning: peak of the large rounded hill
Height: 1099m (3606ft); Rank: 51
OS Landranger Map 41
Summit grid ref: NN164667 (cairn on rock)

Munros. The middle four are known as The Ring of Steall.

It's a fabulous day out – a thrilling mountain adventure, and one to savour in good conditions. It includes a walk through a stunning gorge, a river crossing on a wire bridge, excellent stalkers' paths, fine, airy ridge walking, fun scrambling and awe-inspiring views of some of the country's most famous mountains – including the Grey Corries, the Aonachs and Ben Nevis. Oh, and you pass beneath the second-highest waterfall in Scotland!

The first time I attempted the route was in April one year. We walked it clockwise and the day started well enough – weather was slightly overcast but fine. After the second Munro, Stob Coire a' Chairn, a vicious late winter storm struck. Snow and fog meant visibility was at times appalling, but it was the wind that really caused us alarm – it was ferocious, and any movement was a struggle.

On the narrow ridge, we were committed with no safe way of descent. With axes and crampons, we battled on over the Munro Am Bodach, and then another peak – the "deleted" Munro Sgor an Iubhair – before we were able to escape to the valley. Sgurr a' Mhaim and the Devil's Ridge had to wait for another day. It was a useful reminder of how fickle the weather can be in Scotland's mountains – and how important it is to have the right equipment and clothing.

THE ROUTE

The route starts at the road end down Glen Nevis, where there's ample parking. It takes in four Munros, An Gearanach, Stob Coire a' Chairn, Am Bodach and Sgurr a' Mhaim.

If a group of you plan this route then having two vehicles would be a bonus – one can be left at Polldubh, to where you descend. It saves a trudge at the end of the day.

The excitement starts almost immediately with a walk through the fabulous Nevis Gorge. The path is rocky and at times narrow, with some big drops on the right. Care is needed.

The gorge opens out to a lovely, grassy, almost alpine meadow that kind of takes you by surprise. At the far end, the mighty Steall Falls are visible, which give this circuit its wonderful pun of a name.

First challenge is crossing the river. The adventurous will do this via the wire bridge, which consists of three cables strung across the burn – one for the feet, two for the hands. It's also possible to ford the river slightly further upstream, at least when the water's low.

From here rocky ground beneath the falls is traversed, then a boggy section to pick up the excellent stalkers' path up the day's first Munro, An Gearanach. The path makes for easy going, zig-zagging in the upper reaches.

From the summit, the way is obvious – the marvellous ridge, often narrow and sometimes requiring simple, but fun, scrambling, links the tops in a long chain.

After Am Bodach is another peak – Sgor an Iubhair. The 1000m (3281ft) summit was promoted to Munro status in 1981, and then demoted following another revision in 1997. Whatever its status, it's a fine peak. Shortly after traversing it, the Devil's Ridge runs north to Sgurr a' Mhaim.

It's a narrow arête, rocky and exposed in places, but should present no real difficulty to those used to a bit of scrambling. In winter it's tougher, and experience is required.

The descent to Polldubh from the last Munro is down its north-west ridge – it's brutally steep. A real knee-buster!

Did You Know?

The great Scottish writer and mountaineer W. H. Murray believed Nevis Gorge to be "the best half-mile in Scotland".

Ben Nevis from An Gearanach

NEVIS GORGE

One of the highlights of the Ring of Steall comes before you even leave the valley floor – the walk through Nevis Gorge.

The 1km (0.6 mile) gorge starts immediately after leaving the car park. The river twists and turns down the very narrow gorge in a series of foaming cascades, with deep turbulent pools after every drop.

The gorge is littered with enormous boulders. Its precipitous walls are pockmarked by great scooped hollows, gouged over centuries by stones and gravel driven by furious waters. Many of the hollows lie surprisingly high on the walls – terrifying testament to how deep the river runs in times of spate. More than once I've heard *The Scots Magazine* columnist and mountaineer Cameron McNeish describe the area as "Himalayan in character, if not scale".

The slopes above are covered in lovely native woods – Scots pine, oak, birch and mountain ash.

An Gearanach, on Ring of Steall

Meall a' Bhuiridh and the River Etive

Did You Know?

The first overhead ski lift on Meall a' Bhuiridh opened in 1956, making the centre now known as Glencoe Mountain the oldest commercial ski area in Scotland.

Meall a' Bhuiridh and Creise

27
Meall a' Bhuiridh

AT 1108m (3635ft) Meall a' Bhuiridh is the highest summit in a fine set of hills known as the Blackmount. There are four Munros in the Blackmount and they neatly divide into sets of two – the northern pairing of Meall a' Bhuiridh and Creise, and in the south Stob Ghabhar and Stob a' Choire Odhair.

Both are good days out, but linking all four gives one of the best hill days around – the Blackmount Traverse, a Scottish mountaineering classic.

It's a testing day, one that only fitter walkers will want to take on. Linking the two sets of hills could be tricky in poor weather, but what an outing!

One of the reasons I recommend it is because, for me, all the skiing infrastructure on Meall a' Bhuiridh kind of spoils that hill as a single, or even, with Creise, as a double Munro outing. The full traverse is so spectacular, it makes up for that.

I fully accept that the ski centre brings employment, provides an enormous tourism boost to the local economy and is a fantastic leisure resource – but the lifts, buildings and bulldozed tracks it requires detract, I feel, from the hill as a walking area, especially in summer when the lack of snow ensures all the infrastructure is exposed. And in winter, it's easy, as a

Pronunciation: *Me-yal a Voo-ray*; Meaning: rounded hill of the bellowing (of rutting stags)
Height: 1108m (3635ft); Rank: 45
OS Landranger Maps 41 & 50
Summit grid ref: NN251503 (cairn)

walker, to feel a bit in the way of all those enjoying the snowsports.

For experienced scramblers who want to avoid the skiing infrastructure, Creise and Meall a' Bhuiridh can be climbed as a pair via Sron na Creise – a tough Grade 2/3 scramble. It's very exposed and loose and not for beginners. Reaching the start of the route involves either a long, pathless walk from the ski centre over boggy, tussocky, heathery ground, or by fording the River Etive – which is not always possible.

One of the highlights of the traverse is the chance to experience Scotland's "other" Aonach Eagach. It's the name given to a short, rocky and occasionally narrow section of ridge on the Munro Stob Ghabhar. It's a very simple, short and fun scrambly section – nowhere near as difficult as its better-known big cousin in Glen Coe.

NEAREST TOWN: Glencoe is around 20km (12.4 miles) north-west. Although a small village it has great facilities. Accommodation options include hotels, B&Bs, caravan and campsites and a youth hostel. There are shops, a petrol station and excellent places to eat and drink. It's also home to the area's mountain rescue team.

RECOMMENDED ROUTE
Start grid ref: NN270418
Distance: 21km (13.1 miles)
Ascent: 2100m (6890ft)
Time: 10hrs

THE ROUTE

Two vehicles make the traverse logistically much simpler. Start the day by leaving a vehicle in the car park at the Glencoe Mountain resort. Then drive round to the car park just short of Victoria Bridge, near the Inveroran Hotel. It's roughly a half-hour drive.

From the car park, cross the bridge and follow the track west alongside the river until you reach the Glasgow University Mountaineering Club hut. Then head north on a boggy path.

The path – an old stalkers' route – improves greatly after the boggy section. It crosses a small river then zig-zags right to the summit of Stob a' Choire Odhair.

West lies the bealach with Stob Ghabhar. Continue west after the low point, before heading up steep ground to the crest of the Aonach Eagach – the path winds up scree and loose rock that requires a little scrambling. The ridge itself runs west and should present no real difficulty – if some exposure.

It joins the Munro's south-east ridge. Climb this to the summit.

From here, north-west then north takes you on to long Aonach Mor ridge. A spur a couple of kilometres along the ridge juts north-east – it leads to the bealach with Clach Leathad. Then it's a very steep climb on what will by now be tired legs to the east ridge of Clach Leathad – a Munro Top of Creise. It's a fine summit in its own right. Creise is only 1km (0.6 miles) north.

Backtrack to the col at 1070m (3510ft),

Rannoch Moor from
Meall a' Bhuiridh

then head east down steep, loose terrain to the bealach with Meall a' Bhuiridh. This section requires a bit of scrambling and care. From the bealach it's a steep pull up rocky ground to the summit of the day's fourth Munro. The descent is just east of north, well to the left of the ski tows.

The final 1km (0.6 miles) or so follows steep ground beneath the ski lift, back to the centre car park.

Buachaille Etive from Meall a' Bhuiridh

SKIING IN SCOTLAND

The Glencoe Mountain ski resort – once known as the White Corries ski centre – has eight lifts and 20 runs on the north-eastern flanks of Meall a' Bhuiridh.

It's a relatively small centre, but enormously popular due to its proximity to Glasgow and the Central Belt – it's barely a two-hour drive from Scotland's biggest city and just 1km (0.6 miles) off the A82 trunk road.

Some lifts carry snowsports enthusiasts almost all the way to the summit of the Munro.

The skiing season in Scotland can sometimes extend into May, but the resort is open year-round. In summer months, it operates mainly as a mountain-biking venue, with downhill and cross-country routes available.

Other activities on offer include tubing – sliding downhill on a giant inflatable ring – and treasure hunting! It has "microlodges" for accommodation and facilities for camping and motorhomes, as well as a cafe and licensed bar.

Blackmount, Rannoch Moor, winter

Aonach Beag

© JOHN McSPORRAN

Aonach Beag and the Carn Mor Arête from Ben Nevis

Did You Know?

Despite "beag" meaning small and "mor" meaning big, Aonach Beag is taller than its neighbour Aonach Mor. The names refer to the mass of the respective hills, rather than height.

28
Aonach Beag

DESPITE being the second-highest mountain in Fort William's Nevis Range – only Ben Nevis is higher – Aonach Beag is quite a secretive hill.

At a bulky 1234m (4049ft), it's the UK's seventh-highest peak, but it's hard to spot, often obscured in roadside views by its near neighbour, the slightly lower Aonach Mor at 1221m (4006ft).

The two Munros are connected by a narrow bealach and are usually climbed as a pair, generally being referred to as "the Aonachs".

The best view of the duo is from the Grey Corries, the range of hills lying immediately to the east and linked to a subsidiary summit of Aonach Beag, Stob Coire Bhealaich, by a col with a low point of 731m (2398ft).

Aonach Mor is the home of the Nevis Range ski centre, so any approach from the north is among the tows and runs, which detract from any feeling of "wildness".

Far better – and the route recommended here – is to approach via Polldubh. It takes in gorgeous little Glen Nevis – Scotland's own miniature version of a Himalayan valley!

The ascent from here, once on the hill, is pathless and – although unremittingly steep in sections – gives a sense of remoteness and solitude.

> Pronunciation: *E-noch Beg*
> Meaning: little ridge
> Height: 1234m (4049ft); Rank: 7
> OS Landranger Map 41
> Summit grid ref: NN196715 (cairn)

As well as being the taller of the two Munros, Aonach Beag is also the finer – Aonach Mor has a much broader summit plateau, so views tend to lack depth.

On ascent of Aonach Beag however, the views of Ben Nevis's north-east face and the Carn Mor Dearg arête in particular appear increasingly impressive – as do those east to the Grey Corries.

The high eastern cliffs of both Aonach Munros hold snow long into summer – patches tend to survive year-round most years – and they're popular winter climbing venues, particularly since the opening of the ski centre, the lifts making access much easier.

The eastern edges of the two Munros can cornice heavily in winter and great care is needed. The cliffs also mean a good level of navigation skill is required in poor visibility – especially at the narrow bealach and on the considerable, featureless plateau of Aonach Mor.

NEAREST TOWN: Fort William is about 10km (6.2 miles) north-west. Scotland's "Outdoor Capital" is well served by public transport. It has supermarkets, gear shops and lots of food, drink and accommodation options. Lochaber Geopark visitor centre, in the town centre, makes for a great visit when the weather's poor.

RECOMMENDED ROUTE
Start grid ref: NN167691
Distance: 16km (9.9 miles)
Ascent: 1480m (4856ft)
Time: 7hrs

THE ROUTE

The most scenic route to Aonach Beag begins at Polldubh, at the end of the public road in Glen Nevis.

From there, head along the fantastic Nevis Gorge – it's a rocky path with some big drops in places.

The path exits the gorge to a wide, flat grassy meadow. Follow the north bank of the Water of Nevis, crossing a bridge to the ruins of Steall Cottage.

A direct ascent north, along the Allt Coire Guibhsachan, can be made but we'll save this path for the descent. A slightly longer but far more attractive route is to head north-east from the ruins. Your target is the ridge that leads to Sgurr a' Bhuic. The grassy slopes are a bit of a slog. They flatten at about 800m (2625ft) before the final pull east to the summit. From there, follow the rim of the crags north-east to a bealach and then ascend to Stob Coire Bhealaich, before the final pull up to the Munro Aonach Beag.

Stony slopes north-west take you in a steep descent to the tiny bealach. From there, easier ground ascends in a little over 1km (0.6 miles) to the summit of Aonach Mor at 1221m (4006ft).

The route of return is tough in poor

Ben Nevis, Aonach Mor, Aonach Beag, the Mamores and the Grey Corries from Stob Coire a' Chearcaill

visibility. Retrace your steps but bear right before the bealach – there's a bit of a path. You want to reach point NN192722 – from there, head west down very steep ground to the bealach with Carn Mor Dearg. Then it's south into Coire Giubhsachan, back to Steall Cottage and out along Nevis Gorge once again.

Buachaille Etive Beag and Aonach Eagach

AONACH MOR

Neighbouring Munro Aonach Mor is a popular venue for skiers.

The sport has been enjoyed on the hill since the 1930s but it was only in 1989 that the centre now known as the Nevis Range – with its formal pistes and gondola – was opened.

The centre has continued to develop over the years and in summer is an incredibly popular – and successful – venue for mountain-bike riders. It's regarded as one of the best mountain-bike courses in the world and hosted the World Mountain Bike World Cup 12 times between 2002 and 2017, as well as the Mountain Bike World Championships in 2007.

The gondola can be used by hillwalkers to access the hillside high on Aonach Mor, from where an easy ascent of Aonach Beag can also be made.

However, such an ascent could only be regarded as cheating by any self-respecting Munro-bagger.

Sgurr Choinnich Mor from Aonach Beag

29
Sgurr Choinnich Mor

Pronunciation: *Sgoor Hoy-nich More*
Meaning: big mossy peak
Height: 1094m (3589ft); Rank: 52
OS Landranger Map 41
Summit grid ref: NN227714 (cairn)

THE Grey Corries is a fabulous long range of hills that snakes along the southern side of the A86 road from Spean Bridge to Roy Bridge.

Sgurr Choinnich Mor isn't the highest of the four Munros that form the sinuous ridge – that honour goes to Stob Choire Claurigh at 1177m (3862ft) – but it's surely the loveliest. It's a fine-edged, shapely pyramid of even proportions – a proper mountain!

The most well-known viewpoint for the Grey Corries is from the Commando Memorial, about 1.6km (1 mile) outside Spean Bridge. It's a wonderful mountain vista, taking in not just the Grey Corries, but the Aonachs and Ben Nevis.

An even better view is from down lonely Glen Roy, accessed from Roy Bridge. From there, the Grey Corries seem to rise from lush native woods of oak and birch, and the quartzite boulders that form the summits, from which the range derives its name, gleam in the sunlight.

The grandest outing in the Grey Corries is the complete traverse of all the Munros. If transport is arranged at either end, the route outlined elsewhere in these pages is a good option.

If not, the walk forms a great horseshoe, starting and finishing at the old tramway south of Corriechoille, where it's possible to leave a vehicle. The most easterly Munro, Stob Ban, can be omitted, allowing for a more manageable round of about 22km (13.7 miles), with 1600m (5249ft) of ascent that will take about nine hours.

However, by that route, Sgurr Choinnich Mor is included only as a there-and-back from Stob Coire an Laoigh. It's a steep descent and re-ascent on legs that will already be tired. The effort will likely be grudged, endured merely for the Munro "tick". It's not something worthy of such a fine peak, so far better to climb the hill from the Glen Nevis side as a single Munro, which is the route recommended here.

Grey Corries

NEAREST TOWN: Spean Bridge is about 10km (6.2 miles) north. It's a village at the junction of the A82 and A86. It has a small selection of shops and places to eat. There's plenty of accommodation options nearby, including the Spean Bridge Hotel. And, of course, the area provides the stunning backdrop for the landmark Commando Memorial.

RECOMMENDED ROUTE
Start grid ref: NN167691
Distance: 16.5km (10.3 miles)
Ascent: 1240m (4068ft)
Time: 7hrs

THE ROUTE

Park at the road end at Polldubh in Glen Nevis and head up the magnificent Nevis Gorge.

As the "danger of death" warning signs suggest it's a rocky path with steep, exposed drops to the gushing river below.

The signs might seem a tad dramatic but there have been accidents here and care should be taken.

The path exits the gorge at a pleasant, green meadow, the towering Falls of Steall looking imposing opposite.

Continue on the north side of the river and across the footbridge to the ruins of Steall Cottage. Leave the path 2km (1.2 miles) beyond the ruins and follow the course of the Allt Coire a' Bhuic, aiming for the col between Stob Coire Bhealaich and Sgurr Choinnich Beag at 731m (2398ft).

Turn right along the bealach, following it to the summit of Sgurr Choinnich Beag, a Munro Top at 963m (3159ft). It's steep and narrow in the upper sections.

Traverse the peak, descending to another col before climbing steeply north-east to the fine summit of Sgurr Choinnich Mor. The views back to the craggy cliffs of the Aonachs are especially impressive.

To return, you can retrace your steps. An alternative that saves a bit of additional

© ANDY SWANSON

ascent is to head back to the ground between the Munro and Sgurr Choinnich Beag – from there it's possible to pick your way back down to the path in Glen Nevis, and then through the gorge to the car park.

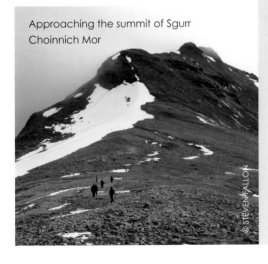
Approaching the summit of Sgurr Choinnich Mor

© STEVEN FALLON

LAIRIG LEACACH BOTHY

At the opposite end of the sinuous ridge that forms the spine of the Grey Corries lies the Lairig Leacach bothy.

It sits at the foot of Stob Ban, the most eastern of the Grey Corries' Munros, and is about a 1.5 hour walk in from the parking area beyond Corriechoille, near Spean Bridge.

Walking in to the tiny bothy to spend the night, before tackling the four Grey Corrie Munros of Stob Ban, Stob Coire Claurigh, Stob Coire an Laoigh and Sgurr Choinnich Mor, turns a long day walk into an adventure! Continue the traverse into Glen Nevis, where ideally you've left a second vehicle at Polldubh.

The bothy, which stands aside an old drove road, has a Dowling stove (you'll have to carry in fuel) and a bunk-bed sleeping platform on to which you could squeeze eight people. Given its proximity to so many fabulous hills, it's a busy bothy year-round.

Beinn nan Aighenan from Clashgour

Descending Beinn nan Aighenan

30
Beinn nan Aighenan

FOR me, Beinn nan Aighenan has to be one of Scotland's most awkward Munros. It's difficult to spell and even harder to pronounce, but toughest of all is just getting to the hill – it's among the most remote in west Scotland.

It's hidden away between Glen Etive and Glen Kinglass, tucked behind its more famous and frequently visited northern neighbours, the Munros Ben Starav and Glas Bheinn Mhor.

It's probably most often climbed – certainly by fitter Munro-baggers – as an addition to these other hills, from the Glen Etive side. It's certainly the route by which I first climbed it. It's a there-and-back from the bealach after Ben Starav if you're tackling the hills anticlockwise from Coileitir. Allow a couple of hours for the extra 4.5km (2.8 miles) and 550m (1805ft) of ascent this will add to your day.

Beinn nan Aighenan is not a hugely distinctive hill. This – along with its remoteness – make me suspect it'd see few walkers if it weren't for that magic Munro status. Its summit is pleasingly rocky on ascent when approached from the north side, but I think the best way up is from Glen Kinglass.

It's a much longer route – but a bike cuts greatly into the distance.

Pronunciation: *Ben Na-naye-na-yan*; Meaning: hill of the hinds
Height: 960m (3150ft); Rank: 196
OS Landranger Map 50
Summit grid ref: NN148405 (cairn)

When combined with its Etive neighbours, these grander, more aesthetically pleasing hills steal the limelight. Beinn nan Aighenan becomes a bit of a hassle, an afterthought – something to be ticked because, well, you're there and you might as well.

From the Glen Kinglass side, however, lonely Beinn nan Aighenan is the star of the show. The other advantage of this route is it avoids the hordes that descend on Glen Etive every weekend. Ben Starav in particular attracts big crowds, meaning parking can be difficult at the start of the route. Driving along Glen Etive's single-track road can also be a challenge when it's so incredibly busy.

While Ben Starav and Glas Bheinn Mhor's slopes are heaving, you're likely to have Beinn nan Aighenan all to yourself.

NEAREST TOWN: Tyndrum is about 20km (12.4 miles) south-east of the summit. The small settlement at the junction of the A82 and A85 has two train stations, a pub, hotel, caravan and camping site and the famous Green Welly Stop, which sells everything from petrol to outdoor gear. For award-wining fish and chips, visit the Real Food Cafe.

RECOMMENDED ROUTE
Start grid ref: NN270418
Distance: 31km (19.3 miles)
Ascent: 1000m (3281ft)
Time: 9hrs

THE ROUTE

Some hill days really call for the use of a bike – this is definitely one of them.

Excellent paths and tracks lead from the public car park just before Victoria Bridge, meaning it's possible to cycle almost all the way to the start of the south-east ridge that will take you to Beinn nan Aighenan's summit.

It'll cut hours off your day. Without a bike, a walk this long on tracks becomes – for me – a bit of a trudge. Albeit a trudge in a beautiful location. I much prefer walking on hills, however, rather than slogging through glens.

From the car park, a track takes you west to Clashgour. Head south for 0.5km (0.3 miles) before turning west again, on another excellent track, all the way past Loch Dochard and into Glen Kinglass. The track runs eventually to Loch Etive and is cycle-able from the east almost to the River Kinglass.

The river is fordable in dry weather. If in spate, there's a bridge at NN185399.

Almost as soon as you're across the river, start ascending the long south-east ridge, the route of which will have been well seen on your approach.

It's initially quite a steep slog but a fine way to ascend the hill – once the broad ridge is gained, the route undulates over a few minor lumps. It feels wonderfully remote and lonely country.

From the summit, return by the route of ascent – and make sure you remember where you left your bike!

Glen Kinglass from Beinn nan Aighenan

THE INVERORAN HOTEL

The road into Victoria Bridge car park takes you past the historic Inveroran Hotel. It's right on the West Highland Way, and a popular stop-off point for walkers.

The building has a long history and was once a drovers' inn. It dates from 1708 and has welcomed a number of surprisingly famous visitors in its time.

Among them was Charles Darwin, who's said to have developed some of his writings on natural selection after studying birch trees in the area.

Charles Dickens was another visitor. Not all enjoyed their experience, however. Poet siblings William and Dorothy Wordsworth complained that their breakfast oatcakes and boiled eggs were as hard as stones, while the butter was inedible.

Thankfully, the current proprietors offer a much tastier selection of restaurant and bar meals, as well as excellent accommodation. The refurbished Walkers' Bar is a welcome oasis after a hard day on the hill.

Looking north west from Liathach's fearsome ridge

NORTHERN
HIGHLANDS

Gairloch

Liathach ▲

Torridon

Beinn
Liath
Mhor ▲

Lochcarron

Portree

Skye

Raasay

Kyle of   *Lochs Duich,*
Lochalsh   *Long and*   Dornie
           Alsh Marine
           Protected
           Area

Bla Bheinn
▲

Sgurr Dubh Mor
▲

The Five Sisters of Kintail ▲

Ullapool

Bonar Bridge

An Teallach

Beinn Dearg ▲

Ben Wyvis ▲

Fionn Bheinn
▲

Garve

Dingwall

Achnasheen

Beauly

Inverness

Cannich

Mam
Sodhail ▲

Bla Bheinn from the eastern approach

Did You Know?

Folklore says Loch na Sguabaidh, near Bla Bheinn, was the home of a kelpie, said to have been killed by a Mackinnon at the Bealach na Beiste – the Pass of the Beast – that separates the hills of Garbh Bheinn and Belig.

Bla Bheinn from Loch Slapin

31

Bla Bheinn

A N outlier of the Cuillin, Bla Bheinn is regarded by many as the finest mountain on Skye.

Often anglicised to "Blaven", it's the only one of the island's 12 Munros not on the main Cuillin ridge.

It's separated from the rest of the group by Strath na Creitheach, and its isolation means it can be appreciated as a single mountain, rather than a complex mass of jagged peaks like the main ridge.

With its separation and distinctive outline, Bla Bheinn stand out in many views and is easily identifiable from a considerable way – even from distant mainland mountains.

Bla Bheinn's distance from the rest of the Cuillin makes it perhaps the best viewpoint on the island for the main range – it looks close enough to touch but is far away enough to give a proper sense of perspective.

It's a great viewpoint, too, for the Red Hills – or Red Cuillin as they're sometimes known. They're beautiful hills themselves, but much smaller and far more rounded than their more dramatic cousins.

One of the best days out on Skye is the Clach Glas–Bla Bheinn traverse. It's a graded climb – a "Moderate" by the easiest line – so rock climbing and abseiling skills are necessary. There's no walking route on

Pronunciation: *Blah Ven*
Meaning: blue hill
Height: 928m (3045ft); Rank: 252
OS Landranger Map 32
Summit grid ref: NG530217 (cairn)

Clach Glas – a sheer blade of rock linked to the main summit by a ridge – and its summit is a real prize.

Bla Bheinn is a popular hill – more accessible and an easier climb than the other Cuillin peaks. The "normal" route, which I recommend here, is from a car park near the head of Loch Slapin. It makes for a relatively short day, and although "easier" than other Cuillin summits, it's still a challenge – very rocky with a little bit of scrambling required. It's a superb introduction to the Cuillin.

Bla Bheinn

Bla Bheinn from Torrin

NEAREST TOWN: Broadford is 11km (6.8 miles) or so east. It has a selection of shops, a petrol station, chippy, restaurants and cafes. It also has a youth hostel and other accommodation. Broadford Hotel is famous as the home of the Drambuie liqueur, from a recipe said to be handed over by Bonnie Prince Charlie himself . . .

RECOMMENDED ROUTE
Start grid ref: NG560215
Distance: 8km (5 miles)
Ascent: 940m (3084ft)
Time: 5hrs

THE ROUTE

There's a car park on the B8083 road from Broadford. It's on the western shore at the head of Loch Slapin, on the right-hand side just over the bridge on the Allt na Dunaiche.

An excellent path leads along the north bank of the burn, above an attractive gorge with tumbling waterfalls and beautiful woods.

The route follows the river, crossing it before climbing into the Coire Uaigneich – which translates as "the secret corrie". You'll reach a flatter, grassy area, while overhead loom Bla Bheinn's great cliffs.

From here, the route skirts the cliffs and climbs north-north-west in steep zig-zags, on the grass flank at first, and then scree and rock on the south-east ridge, passing the famous rock tower known as the Great Prow.

More level ground is reached at a shoulder, from where the going is much more straightforward. The ridge narrows and a short, undemanding scramble leads to the summit.

CUILLIN MOUNTAINS

Skye's Cuillin mountains are the nearest we get in the UK to an alpine ridge.

The spectacular range – of which Bla Bheinn is an outlier – curves for some 14km (8.7 miles) around Loch Coruisk.

It contains 11 Munros and nine Tops – summits of Munro height but not considered separate mountains.

The Cuillin – including Bla Bheinn – are made of rock called gabbro. It's incredibly rough, which makes it great for scrambling – you almost stick to it! It also makes it very hard-wearing on boots, clothing and skin… a day scrambling with no gloves will leave your fingers red, sore and probably bleeding.

The mountain chain is all that remains of a giant volcano, which was active some 60 million years ago. On some parts of the ridge, the rock has unusual magnetic qualities that can interfere with compass needles, giving misleading information. A high level of map-reading skill is required for those venturing into the Cuillin without a guide.

All around are spectacular views – it's a thrilling vista. The easiest route of descent is to reverse the ascent.

Reflections of Bla Bheinn

Looking south from the Inaccessible Pinnacle towards Sgurr Thearlaich and Sgurr Dubh Mor

En route to the summit from the east

Did You Know?

On June 16, 2013, hill runner and climber Finlay Wild set a new record for the traverse of the entire Cuillin – an incredible 3hrs 14mins 58s. Incredibly he then beat this four months later on October 12, with a time of 2hrs 59mins 22s.

32
Sgurr Dubh Mor

PEOPLE, usually those not into hillwalking, often ask me *what is your favourite Munro?* It's a hard question to answer, and I used to mumble something about how it depends on the weather, time of year, the company, your mood . . .

And then I climbed Sgurr Dubh Mor in the Skye Cuillin.

I can honestly say, as a single Munro, it's my absolute favourite. Partly it's because conditions were about as good as you could wish for – a dry, sunny day in mid May. No midges, no wind. And the company was great – my good friend Alex MacLennan, with whom I've enjoyed countless days in the hills.

Mostly it's because the whole day was such a fun adventure – starting with a high-speed boat ride from Elgol to Loch Coruisk – and all the while surrounded by the most dramatic and exciting mountain terrain in the UK.

A few years previously we'd traversed the main Cuillin ridge – which is probably my favourite multi-Munro trip – but we'd left out Sgurr Dubh Mor. It's out on a spur, off the main ridge between Sgurr nan Eag and Sgurr Alasdair, and would've added potentially one and a half hours to an already mammoth undertaking.

It also gave us an excuse to return to

Pronunciation: *Sgoor Doo More*
Meaning: big black peak
Height: 944m (3097ft); Rank: 228
OS Landranger Map 32
Summit grid ref: NG457205 (small cairn on rock)

claim our final Skye Munro via a route known as the Dubh Slabs – the longest graded rock climb in the UK.

I hesitated for a long time before making a technical route – "doing the Dubhs" as it's known to climbers – my recommendation for Sgurr Dubh Mor, but I have done so for several reasons.

Firstly, it's the only route by which I've climbed the Munro, so I can't really recommend another.

Secondly, we traversed the hill from Loch Coruisk, crossed the main ridge and finished down at Glen Brittle. So our route of descent could be used in ascent.

Thirdly – although graded a "Moderate" climb – very experienced, competent and confident scramblers should cope fine. Use of a rope might not even be necessary – but one should be carried just in case. A few nuts, hexes and abseil gear are all that's required.

At the top of the slabs, on Sgurr Dubh Beag, is an abseil to a bealach. This can

NEAREST TOWN: Broadford is 19km (11.8 miles) east of the summit. It has numerous accommodation options, including a youth hostel. It also has a petrol station and small supermarket, chip shop, and bars and restaurants. The Broadford Hotel is where the famous Drambuie liqueur was created.

RECOMMENDED ROUTE
Start grid ref: NG486195
Distance: 11km (6.8 miles)
Ascent: 1250m (4101ft)
Time: 9hrs

Loch Coruisk

Looking north-west from the Slabs into Coir' Uisg

apparently be avoided by descending a grassy ledge – but we couldn't see it.

Lastly, the Dubh Slabs is a real Scottish classic – it's hugely enjoyable.

It should be noted that however you ascend Sgurr Dubh Mor, you'll be faced with Grade 2/3 scrambling, considerable drops and complex, rocky terrain requiring very careful route finding.

If in doubt, do not hesitate to hire a guide from one of the many excellent providers on Skye.

THE ROUTE

Two vehicles are pretty much essential for this route – the alternatives involve very long walks in/out on difficult terrain. The route starts from Loch Coruisk, so camping or staying at Camasunary bothy are options.

We left a car in Glen Brittle before driving round to Elgol the following morning to get a high-speed rib to Loch Coruisk.

It's a one-way ticket and you do feel a bit abandoned when the boat roars off. All that lies between you and your car is a 2km (1.2 mile) climb – one of the longest graded routes in Britain – a 26m (85ft) abseil, hard scrambling, the spine of the Cuillin and Coire a' Ghrunnda . . . easy!

A good path leads by the shore of the loch. You can't miss the Dubh Slabs – they form a great rock ramp rising at 30 degrees from the head of the loch.

An obvious – and steep – grassy gully avoids a steep nose at the foot of the slabs. It tops out at a grassy ledge from where a stone chimney takes you to the ridge proper. We pitched this section, as we'd no idea what was above, but it's a straightforward scramble.

The ridge is very wide and formed of the roughest gabbro – you almost stick to it. It's a case of picking your line and padding up. You can make it as easy or tough as you like. Some might like the reassurance of a rope.

Alex MacLennan "doing the Dubhs"

Did You Know?

Loch Coruisk is an anglicisation of the Gaelic "Coire Uisg", meaning *cauldron of waters*. Folklore suggests it's the home of a water horse, commonly known as a kelpie.

About 60m (197ft) or so before the summit of Sgurr Dubh Beag is a small col with a cairn indicating the start of a bypass route to the bealach with Sgurr Dubh Mor. It's on the south side of the ridge apparently. We didn't see it.

Instead, we abseiled from the well-established anchor. It's higher than an older anchor so I'd suggest taking a 60m (197ft) rope. The abseil includes a couple of overhanging sections, and it's not one for a first-timer to try out.

From the bealach, the route now becomes much more like an arête. You'll come to a point where it seems the way is blocked by a great wall of rock – retrace your steps by about 20m (66ft) and there are a series of ledges up which it's possible to scramble. Above this, more exposed scrambling takes you to Sgurr Dubh Mor's summit.

The descent from here is a stiff scramble and requires good route choice down the south face. The aim is to reach the bealach and then scramble up Sgurr Dubh an Da Bheinn. From there, stick to the main ridge for a short distance, heading south-west and then pick your way down to Loch Coir' a' Ghrunnda.

Skirt the south side of the loch before following the outflow into Coire a' Ghrunnda. This will involve more scrambling, but after about 1km (0.6 miles) you'll pick up the excellent track that leads all the way out to Glen Brittle.

THE UNDERWORLD OF SKYE

Elgol's not just where you get the boat that takes you to the heart of the Cuillin – it's also the place from where you can explore Skye's hidden underworld . . .

Spar Cave is one of Scotland's subterranean wonders. It lies close to Glasnakille, around 2km (1.2 miles) east of Elgol on a winding single track.

The huge cavern is 50m (164ft) long, with cathedral-like grandeur – the walls and floor are covered in "spar", or flowstone as it's also known.

It forms marble-like "staircases" which carry you deep into the interior – it looks slippy but is actually very grippy.

Made of calcium carbonate deposited from centuries of water trickling through limestone, the flowstone also forms great pillars. Once there were many stalactites, but Victorian visitors removed them as souvenirs. In places, the walls and roof are stained by soot from the torches and candles they carried. The caves can only be visited at low tide – check times online or locally, otherwise you could be trapped for 12 hours.

Did You Know?

Near Liathach lies the village of Shieldaig. It was founded in 1800 as a training post for sailors during the Napoleonic Wars. It was later a fishing village.

On Liathach's ridge

33
Spidean a' Choire Leith (Liathach)

I RECKON the first thought most hillwalkers have when they initially catch sight of Liathach is: *How on earth am I going to climb that?*

More than any other Scottish mountain, it looks utterly impregnable. It's a vast lump of a hill, intimidatingly steep. End to end, the mountain stretches for 7km (4.4 miles) – and a finer, more exhilarating 7km you will not find in Britain.

Liathach actually has two Munros. Spidean a' Choire Leith is the highest and lies toward the eastern end of the mountain. The western peak – Mullach an Rathain – was only promoted to Munro status in 1981.

Like the other Torridon mountains, Liathach seems to thrust almost directly from sea level to Munro height. All the hills here sit apart from one another, great solitary giants rising from the plains below.

The lands here are sparsely populated and roads are single track. The area gives a sensation of remoteness, wildness. More than that though, it feels old – a feeling of age that goes beyond the mere centuries or even millennia of human understanding. It's ancient – primeval. The bedrock here is among the oldest rock on the planet, but even without that knowledge, the sense of that tremendous age somehow permeates the area.

Pronunciation: *Speed-yan a Cor-ye Lay (Lee-ach)*; Meaning: peak of the grey corrie (the grey one)
Height: 1055m (3461ft); Rank: 75
OS Landranger Map 25
Summit grid ref: NG929580 (cairn)

Liathach has a claim as the most visually stunning of all Scotland's mountains – and it's a hard claim to contest. Torridon is the most incredible place for hillwalkers in Britain – and Liathach is arguably the finest of the area's mountains.

It's perfectly possible to climb the two Munros and omit the ridge between – but to do that would be to forego one of the greatest mountaineering days the UK has to offer. The traverse of Liathach is a Scottish mountaineering classic – and I'd urge anyone with appropriate scrambling experience to do it. It is marvellous.

It's a thrilling day out. At times it's a Grade 2 scramble but most of the difficulties can be bypassed if need be. Far below the ridge runs a path that bypasses all the scrambling – but from what I saw when I did the route, it looks more precarious than sticking to the ridge.

My advice, pick your weather and enjoy it!

NEAREST TOWN: Torridon is a little over 4km (2.5 miles) west. It's a small village and facilities are limited, but there's an excellent youth hostel and a shop/cafe. The nearby Torridon Inn is very popular and serves high-quality food.

RECOMMENDED ROUTE
Start grid ref: NG935566
Distance: 11.5km (7.2 miles)
Ascent: 1330m (4364ft)
Time: 8hrs

THE ROUTE

The full traverse of Liathach – taking in Munros Spidean a' Choire Leith and Mullach an Rathain – is a day in the mountains never to be forgotten.

It's finer, I believe, then even An Teallach or the Aonach Eagach. Sure, it's not as committing as the Aonach Eagach in the sense that many of the harder sections can be bypassed, but the grandeur of Liathach's situation – near the coast with the other Torridon giants all around – lifts it to another level entirely.

There's a layby just off the A896 Glen Torridon road, about 0.5km (0.3 miles) east of Glen Cottage. From here, an excellent path winds its way steeply alongside the Allt an Doire Ghairbh to the corrie of Toll a' Meitheach. It includes some minor sections of scrambling – but nothing compared to what lies ahead.

From the corrie, the path steepens markedly until the ridge is gained up, just west of Stuc a' Choire Dhuibh Bhig, up a scree gully. Most sources suggest detouring to this, Liathach's most eastern summit, and I have to say I agree – the views of Beinn Eighe are incredible, plus it's quite pleasing to do the entire ridge.

Retrace your steps to the bealach and then over the two very stony tops of Stob a' Choire Liath Mhor before the bouldery peaked summit of Spidean a' Choire Leith – it's rough going.

The whole of the rest of the route is now visible – 2km (1.2 miles) of twisting, sinuous narrow ridge and a series of shattered pinnacles – Am Fasarinen – that bite into the sky like great, jagged teeth. It's sensational!

The scramble over the pinnacles is a solid Grade 2 in places. It's exposed and any fall is likely to be fatal – the drops are considerable. The rock, however, is excellent and grippy – it's made for scrambling. There are also easier options on most of the difficulties, but prior scrambling experience to a decent level and a good head for heights are essential.

There is a bypass path below, but it is very eroded in sections – especially over some deep gullies – looks slippy and is itself very exposed. It looks sketchier than the pinnacles to be honest.

After the final pinnacle, the ridge broadens to a grassy slope that leads without further difficulty to Mullach an Rathain at 1023m (3356ft) – it too is a fine viewpoint, especially for Beinn Alligin.

To descend, head south-west on a stony path to a shoulder, where a zig-zagging path leads down steep and eroded scree slopes.

The route improves but involves a couple of rocky sections where it cuts through stone terraces. Eventually it takes you out to the roadside – it's then about 2km (1.2 miles) east back to the car.

Liathach at dawn

Did You Know?

Liathach's famous – or infamous – pinnacles are known as "Am Fasarinen", which translates from Gaelic as "The Teeth".

TORRIDONIAN SANDSTONE

The rocks and mountains of Torridon played an important role in the development of the geological sciences in the 18th and 19th centuries.

Indeed, the rock that Liathach and the neighbouring mountains are formed of is now known as "Torridonian sandstone". The term was coined in the Victorian era by Scots geologist James Nicol. Laid down in ancient times in sedimentary bands and transformed by heat and pressure, the sandstone layers are clearly visible on the mountains – like great stone terraces.

The mountains of Torridon are among the oldest in the UK, dating from perhaps 60 million years ago – older than the Alps and Himalayas.

The rock they lie upon – Lewisian Gneiss – is among the oldest known on earth at more than 2.5 billion years old.

Countless millennia of wind, ice and frost have carved the sandstone into wondrous shapes – it's also excellent for scrambling on, being very grippy.

View to Mullach an Rathain

Beinn Liath Mhor's hump-backed ridge

The eastern top of Beinn Liath Mhor

Did You Know?

Many mountain bikers regard the descent from the head of Coire Lair back to Achnashellach as the finest section of downhill track for riding in the UK.

34
Beinn Liath Mhor

AS its name says, Beinn Liath Mhor is indeed a big grey hill. It lies in the rough, mountainous country between Glen Carron and Glen Torridon.

Sparsely populated and with dramatic scenery on a grand scale, this feels like untamed territory – very much Scotland's Wild West.

From the Glen Carron side, the circular route around Coire Lair – taking in the Munros of Beinn Liath Mhor, Sgorr Ruadh and the Corbett Fuar Tholl – is one of the finest mountain days in the area.

It's a long, tiring day over challenging ground however – 16.5km (10.3 miles) with 1700m (5577ft) of ascent and will take about nine hours.

Here, I describe taking in Beinn Liath Mhor as a single Munro. The route takes in arguably the best part of the longer circuit – the fabulous undulating high-level summit ridge of Beinn Liath Mhor. It runs for more than 2km (1.2 miles) over three big humps and never drops below 800m (2625ft). Underfoot, on grass and quartzite stones, the going's very easy – it's a delight to walk.

All around are the most exhilarating views of some of the finest mountains in the whole of Britain. I recommend walking it anticlockwise – that way the mighty Torridon giants of Liathach and Beinn Eighe lure you on.

Pronunciation: *Ben Leea Vore*
Meaning: big grey hill
Height: 926m (3038ft); Rank: 258
OS Landranger Map 25
Summit grid ref: NG964519 (large cairn)

On a fine day, it really is breathtaking stuff. Gazing north-west from the summit, Beinn Alligin rises straight from the sea. Your eyes drift east over the Liathach's fearsome Am Fasarinen pinnacles, then the great silvery brute of Beinn Eighe – beyond that, you can even make out the wickedly serrated outline of An Teallach. It's like a mountain that's exploded into the sky.

Get the right day and you won't want it to end – fitter walkers will certainly want to add on one or both the hills mentioned above.

It's a bit of a slog up very steep slopes to reach Beinn Liath Mhor's ridge – but here too the views more than compensate for the effort.

Dominant is the incredible outline of Fuar Tholl – its great cliffs and Mainreachan Buttress are famous winter climbing venues. Many regard the hill – which misses Munro status by just 7m (22ft) – as one of the finest, if not the finest, Corbetts in Scotland.

NEAREST TOWN: Strathcarron is around 14km (8.7 miles) south-east. It's a small hamlet but it does have a railway station, there's a campsite nearby and the Strathcarron Hotel does a nice pint. Before Strathcarron lies Achnashellach, and the legendary Gerry's Hostel.

RECOMMENDED ROUTE
Start grid ref: NH005483
Distance: 15km (9.3 miles)
Ascent: 1050m (3445ft)
Time: 6.5hrs

THE ROUTE

There's a sizeable layby on the south of the A890 road, opposite a telephone box and the start of the small private road that leads to Achnashellach Station.

Head to the station and over the railway line at the crossing point. A good track takes you to a junction – turn left and follow the forest road. After a few hundred metres, a marker post indicates a path right – follow it through a gate and then turn right, along the River Lair.

The path climbs into the Coire Lair – ignore a left-hand branch but head 100m (328ft) further to a junction marked by a cairn. Take the right fork.

This branch would eventually lead to Loch Coulin but we leave it at the high point, after just a few hundred metres. On the left, a path crosses a boulder-strewn slope to reach Beinn Liath Mhor's broad ridge. It's a steep, energy-sapping slog at times.

The ground eases to the east top. It has an enormous, well-built cairn, but at just 876m (2874ft) don't be fooled into thinking this is the summit. That lies just north of

192

west, some 2km (1.2 miles) away over the marvellous, undulating ridge.

After enjoying the extensive views from the true summit, continue along the ridge to a shoulder – from here the descent to Bealach Coire Lair is rather awkward. It'd be quite difficult in poor weather.

A small cairn marks the start of a path that leads first down a stone gully. Pick your way to the bealach, where you'll cross an old stalkers' path. Turn left along this and down into Coire Lair. It leads back to the junction with your inward route. From there, retrace your steps back to Achnashellach.

Did You Know?

Achnashellach Railway Station was opened in 1870. In 1892, a brake failure resulted in a runaway train colliding with another there, resulting in several injuries.

View into Torridon from Beinn Liath Mhor

BATTLES AND TRAINS

The route to Beinn Liath Mhor starts at Achnashellach, where in 1505 Highlanders are said to have fought a fierce clan battle.

The details are very sketchy, but it seems a group of Camerons took on and beat a combined force of Mackays and Munros. A noted casualty of the battle was Sir William Munro of Foulis, a "Justiciary and Lieutenant of Inverness and the Earldom of Ross".

Today Achnashellach, which translates from Gaelic as "the field of the willows", consists of an unstaffed railway station and several houses hidden by forest. The station operates as a "request" stop – meaning you have to ask the guard to get the conductor to halt the train if you want to get off. If you want to get on the train at the platform, you stick out your arm as if hailing a taxi.

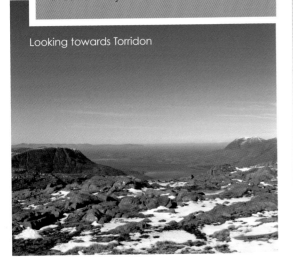
Looking towards Torridon

Did You Know?

An Teallach's overhanging and most fearsome pinnacle is called Lord Berkley's Seat. The peer is said to have sat there and enjoyed his pipe while dangling his legs into the abyss.

Mountain ridge leading to An Teallach

35

Bidein a' Ghlas Thuill (An Teallach)

S An Teallach the finest of Scotland's mountains? It's an assertion that's hard to refute.

The grand mountain rises out of the moor south of Dundonnell and Little Loch Broom.

It has two Munros – Bidein a' Ghlas Thuill is the highest at 1062m (3484ft); the other, Sgurr Fiona, is slightly lower at 1060m (3478ft) and was only promoted to Munro status in 1981.

But there's more to An Teallach than just that – much more . . . it has eight other summits over 914m (2999ft). Half are tightly clustered in a narrow, precipitous ridge that curves south-east from Sgurr Fiona for 2km (1.2 miles).

They form a castellated, broken crest with towers of rock thrusting at all angles into the sky and overhanging the corrie far below – it's an explosion of Tolkienesque peaks.

The traverse of An Teallach is among the very best of mountain days in Scotland – arguably only bettered by Skye's Cuillin.

I think Liathach slightly edges out An Teallach in the aesthetic stakes – but there's more to a mountain than mere looks. The scrambling on An Teallach is far harder and more sustained than on both Liathach and the Aonach Eagach.

Those who aren't keen on scrambling will be pleased to know that it's possible

Pronunciation: *Bid-yin a Glas Hool (An Cha-lach)*; Meaning: peak of the green-grey hollow (the forge)
Height: 1062m (3484ft); Rank: 72
OS Landranger Map 19
Summit grid ref: NH069844 (cairn)

to simply walk to both Munro summits. Even the traverse of the mountain can be completed – just about – by walking. There's a bypass path on the west side, beneath the crest – it's rather eroded in sections though, and there are a couple of sketchier parts that are quite exposed.

If you're uncomfortable on such ground, a there-and-back from Dundonnell is the best option.

Scramblers, however, will have a day they'll never forget.

Most books seem to recommend an anticlockwise route, starting at Corrie Hallie and initially following the path that leads to Shenavall bothy – which is also a good base for the hill for those looking for an overnighter.

I've traversed the mountain in both directions and I prefer the approach from Dundonnell, for the simple reason that the view when you summit Bidein a' Ghlas Thuill is incredible, among the best in Scotland.

NEAREST TOWN: Dundonnell, almost 5km (3.1 miles) north-east, is not exactly what you'd call a town. There is a bunkhouse nearby and numerous B&Bs. The Dundonnell Hotel is an excellent base, with great food and beer. Campers and campervanners are welcome to pitch up free if you buy a meal.

RECOMMENDED ROUTE
Start grid ref: NH093879
Distance: 15.6km (9.7 miles)
Ascent: 1485m (4872ft)
Time: 8hrs

Ahead is the sharp pyramid of Sgurr Fiona; beyond that the rocky towers and jumbled peaks of the ridge. No matter how many times you've climbed it, it's a sight that sets the pulse racing and gives a twinge of anticipation for the day to come.

THE ROUTE

Start from the large parking area a few hundred metres east of the Dundonnell Hotel.

If possible, leave a second vehicle at Corrie Hallie – where the walk's outward path regains the road. It will save a 4km (2.5 mile) trek on tarmac at the end of the day when your legs are tired and feet sore.

Head east along the road for a very short distance to a path that leads to the right. It climbs quickly and steeply south-west in a series of zig-zags up Meall Garbh. After a brief respite, the path climbs again – more gently this time – to Sron a' Choire.

The route now swings south-east to a col just below Bidein a' Ghlas Thuill. A steep, increasingly narrow and stony ridge leads to the summit – the view to Sgurr Fiona and the Corrag Buidhe pinnacles is mind-blowing.

The way to Sgurr Fiona is obvious on a clear day – follow the crest of the narrow, rocky ridge south-west to the bealach and then steeply to the summit. The direct scramble to the summit is easy enough but there's also a scree path.

Now comes the fun part of the day – the wonderful scramble over the pinnacles. There are paths that bypass all difficulties – these also involve a bit of exposure. It's far better, I think, to stick to the rock. Most guide books describe it as a "tough scramble". Nowhere is it ever hugely difficult for experienced scramblers, and it's on great rock with plenty of holds. It's a solid Grade 2 in parts.

I've seen parties roped up, moving together but it's not necessary. The far end of the Corrag Buidhe is a graded rock climb ("Moderate") and should not be attempted without appropriate equipment – backtrack slightly and you can pick your way down a gulley to regain the path.

The scrambling finishes all too quickly. The rest of the day is a walk, taking you over Cadha Gobhlach and Sail Liath. From here head south-east then east, aiming for the south end of Lochan na Brathan, beyond which is the excellent path that leads from Corrie Hallie to Shenavall. Follow the track north-east back to the road.

Scrambling on An Teallach

DESTITUTION ROAD

A famous view of An Teallach is from the A832 road, on approach from Braemore Junction.

The huge mountain rears up from open moorland, its splayed, jagged pinnacles tearing into the sky.

It's an awe-inspiring sight – particularly the pinnacles, and especially if you're heading there with the knowledge you'll soon be climbing them.

With such an attention-grabbing view, few will give much thought to the road on which they travel. Its past, however, marks a sad chapter in the history of the Highlands.

The section from Braemore Junction to Dundonnell is known as Destitution Road, one of several across the Highlands.

It was built by starving crofting families, for food, under the direction of the Central Board for the Destitute Highlands in the late 1840s after the potato crop failed. The families worked eight hours a day, six days a week. Men got 680g (1.5lb) of oatmeal per day, women half that and children 230g (0.5lb).

Five Sisters from above Glen Shiel

Did You Know?

The five peaks collectively known as The Five Sisters of Kintail include three Munros – Sgurr Fhuaran, 1067m (3501ft); Sgurr na Ciste Duibhe, 1027m (3369ft) and Sgurr na Carnach, 1002m (3287ft).

Five Sisters from the slopes of Sgurr na Sgine

36

Sgurr Fhuaran (The Five Sisters of Kintail)

THE classic view of The Five Sisters of Kintail – of which Sgurr Fhuaran is the highest – is from a layby on the Glenelg road as it climbs steeply through Ratagan Forest.

They form a vast mountain wall, the five shapely, pointed peaks surging vertiginously from the waters of Loch Duich. It's no wonder the original Gaelic name for the range was simply Bheinn Mhor – "big mountain".

The sheer scale of the mountains in this part of Glen Shiel – particularly those on the north side which include the Sisters – is something to behold. I can't think of anywhere else in Scotland where hills of such bulk rise so steeply from so close to the roadside. The effect – especially on a gloomy day full of foreboding – can be quite intimidating.

The Five Sisters and much of the surrounding area – including the spectacular Falls of Glomach – is owned by the National Trust for Scotland, and were purchased for the nation in 1944.

From the east, the Five Sisters are Sgurr na Ciste Duibhe (Munro), Sgurr na Carnach (promoted to Munro status in 1997), Sgurr Fhuaran (Munro), Sgurr nan Saighead and Sgurr na Moraich. The traverse – usually completed from east to west – is one of the Scottish

> Pronunciation: *Sgoor Oor-an*
> Meaning: possibly peak of the spring, or peak of the wolf
> Height: 1067m (3501ft); Rank: 70
> OS Landranger Map 33
> Summit grid ref: NG978167 (cairn)

mountaineering classics and the route I recommend.

Most walkers will want to climb the Munros at least, and it's possible to descend from Sgurr Fhuaran's north-west ridge. It's a long, punishing descent however, and if the River Shiel is impassable it's a rough, pathless walk to Shiel Bridge.

Far better is to carry on over the fine peak of Sgurr nan Saighead – perhaps the most exciting hill in the group. The descent to Ault a' Chruinn can be made from the north-west ridge of Beinn Bhuidhe but purists will want to continue to the fifth Sister, Sgurr na Moraich.

If possible, it's a good idea to leave a vehicle at Ault a' Chruinn as you're now 12km (7.5 miles) by road from your start point.

Sgurr Fhuaran (Five Sisters) and Glen Shiel

NEAREST TOWN: Shiel Bridge is 5km
(3.1 miles) north-west of the summit.
Facilities are limited but there is
a campsite, and hotels, inns and
places to eat in the surrounding
area. There's a youth hostel nearby
at Ratagan.

RECOMMENDED ROUTE
Start grid ref: NH005136
Distance: 12km (7.5 miles)
Ascent: 1600m (5249ft)
Time: 9hrs

THE ROUTE

There's a decent-sized parking area on
the north-side of the A87 road down Glen
Shiel. It's near the site of the Battle of Glen
Shiel and directly below the Bealach an
Lapain.

And it's the bealach that's the first target
of the day. From the parking area, climb
alongside an area of forestry – the slope is
very steep, very wet and unrelenting. The
bealach is at 725m (2379ft) and it'll be a
relief to reach it.

The route lies west and is obvious on
a clear day – a twisting ridge of grass and
rock, wonderfully narrow in places, that
rises and falls into the distance.

A couple of tops are traversed – the first
being Sgurr nan Spainteach – before the
Munro of Sgurr na Ciste Duibhe, 1027m
(3369ft) is climbed.

The second Munro, the 1002m
(3287ft) Sgurr na Carnach, is reached by
descending west then north-west to the
Bealach na Craoibhe, from where the
summit is a short ascent north.

Sgurr Fhuaran is a highlight of the day.
First descend north to the Bealach na
Carnach then climb a steeply zig-zagging
path to the summit.

Continue over Sgurr nan Saighead – a
fine, pointy, rocky peak that gives the
airiest feeling of exposure you'll get all day.

The narrow ridge continues to Beinn
Bhuidhe. Those with the energy will stick

Did You Know?

At the Battle of Glen Shiel in 1719, the British Army used the portable "coehorn" mortar bomb for the first time.

with the ridge, descending first north-east then climbing north-west, to the final Sister, Sgurr na Moraich.

From the summit, head along the north-west ridge for several hundred metres from where a steep descent can be made to a path above the Allt a' Chruinn, which can then be followed out to Ault a' Chruinn.

On the Fives Sisters' ridge

SGURR NAN SPAINTEACH

The first peak traversed en route to the Five Sisters is called Sgurr nan Spainteach, or "peak of the Spaniards".

It's named in honour of Spanish troops who fought alongside Jacobites against the British Army at the Battle of Glen Shiel – the culmination, and only battle, of the 1719 uprising.

The battle, on June 10, saw around 1000 Jacobites and perhaps 300 Spanish soldiers defeated by a contingent of British Government redcoats – mostly Scottish troops – led by General Joseph Wightman. It's the last engagement between foreign and British troops on UK soil.

The Spaniards were an advance party for an invasion fleet carrying some 5000 soldiers from Spain. As with the Armada more than a century previously, bad weather wrecked the ships.

Following the defeat, the Spanish troops fled over the mountain that's now named after them.

The outlaw Rob Roy Macgregor also fought for the Jacobite cause at the battle.

Beinn Dearg from Cona' Mheall

The west ridge of Beinn Dearg

Did You Know?

Beinn Dearg lies on one of the narrowest parts of Scotland – from the saltwater Loch Broom in the west to the Dornoch Firth is just 43.5km (27 miles).

37
Beinn Dearg

THE highest peak in the Northern Highlands, Beinn Dearg is a fine big lump of a hill, dominating views south-east from Ullapool.

It's part of a fairly compact group of four Munros most easily accessed from Inverlael. The others are Cona' Mheall, Meall nan Ceapraichean and Eididh nan Clach Geala. A bit of a mouthful for non-Gaelic speakers and most hillwalkers refer to them simply as "the Deargs".

As a single hill, Beinn Dearg can be climbed via the forest trails from Inverlael, and then the excellent stalkers' path to Bealach an Lochain Uaine. From there, the famine wall can be followed, diverting to the summit. The wall can be followed once again down the west ridge – which steepens considerably toward its end. It makes a nice loop. Cona' Mheall can be added as a there-and-back.

However, the best day out on Beinn Dearg – and the route I recommend – is the circuit of all four Munros. It's a fantastic day out in country that feels very wild. Views north from the bealach and the hilltops in particular are into incredibly remote country – in UK terms at least. There's barely a sign of human activity.

North lies the pointy peak of Seana Bhraigh – one of the hardest to reach of all Munros. It looks deceptively close. Many

Pronunciation: *Ben Ger-ag*
Meaning: red hill
Height: 1084m (3556ft): Rank: 57
OS Landranger Map 20
Summit grid ref: NH259812 (large cairn)

do include it in this round of hills – but that's a truly mammoth expedition. Best to leave it for another day – or even a camp.

I've walked this round of four summer and winter – it's a superb day, whatever the time of year. It's a big day though – my winter round took just over nine hours so I'd recommend waiting for the longer days of March, when the snow can be crisp underfoot and the sun blazing overhead, unless you don't mind starting or finishing in the dark.

One August when I did this round, we met a lone Austrian woman at Bealach an Lochain Uaine. She'd seen us heading back from Cona' Mheall and waited. Thick clag shrouded the summits and she told us she wanted to do Beinn Dearg but that it was "too dark".

Instead, the woman asked if she could tag along with us on our final two Munros of the day. We were more than happy but were stunned to discover she had a map but no compass.

River Lael below the cliffs of Beinn Dearg

My friend Ron asked if she used a compass on the hills back home. "No," she answered. "In Austria we can see our mountains."

THE ROUTE

As well as Beinn Dearg, this route takes in Cona' Mheall, 978m (3209ft), Meall nan Ceapraichean, 977m (3205ft) and Eididh nan Clach Geala, 927m (3041ft).

There's a large parking area next to a red phone box and buildings off the A835, on the right-hand side just before Inverlael Bridge as you approach from the south.

Hardcore tracks take you through Inverlael Forest. Keep on the main track, which takes you over a bridge after about 2km (1.2 miles).

The forest track ends at a turning area and a gate, from where you pick up an excellent stalkers' path. This takes you to lovely little Lochan Lathail with its tiny island. Beyond this, it zig-zags up to Bealach na Lochain Uaine.

Head south-east across sometimes boggy ground to the massive famine wall. This runs up the shoulder of Beinn Dearg. There's a gap in the wall near the top, where the wall suddenly turns right. The massive summit cairn is a couple of hundred metres south-south-west.

Retrace your steps back to the bealach. Cona' Mheall is a there-and-back and there's a path initially. It fades a bit but appears again later as you zig-zag up the stony slopes. The views into the wilds of Sutherland from the summit are marvellous. It feels truly remote.

Again, head back to Bealach na Lochain Uaine. From the lochan, it's a steady pull north-west up a fine ridge that leads to Meall nan Ceapraichean's summit. Head over the lower summit of Ceann Garbh. Head east from here for a couple of hundred metres until the ground levels – then pick your way north-east down steep slopes and craggy ground to the boggy bealach. This section requires great care in winter when the steep slopes are covered in ice and snow.

From the bealach, it's a short climb north-west up steep, grassy slopes to the summit of Eididh nan Clach Geala.

Leave the summit via the west ridge almost as far as the lochan named as Sidhean Dubh on maps. From here, a steep descent south leads to a stalkers' path that takes you west and joins the inward route.

Path below Beinn Dearg with Beinn Eighe in the distance

THE FAMINE WALL

A great drystone wall runs for several miles from the bealach up the eastern flank of Beinn Dearg, over the summit plateau and down the long west ridge.

It's a phenomenal piece of engineering, constructed from tremendous blocks of stone and in places is almost two metres (6ft) tall.

It's known as a "famine wall" and is part of the often sad history of the people who once scraped a living in the shadow of the hills where today so many spend their leisure time.

The wall was built in the 1840s, when disease ravaged the potato crops in Ireland and – as perhaps is less well known – the Highlands.

All across the Highlands, destitute, starving crofters were put to work on projects like Beinn Dearg's famine wall in return for a handout of food. Often, the works had no practical purpose – the idea was that those in receipt of "charity" had to do something to earn their handout.

Ben Wyvis at sunset

Ben Wyvis

38
Glas Leathad Mor (Ben Wyvis)

THE enormous Ben Wyvis sprawls like a sleeping elephant, dominating the skyline north of Inverness.

It's a solitary mountain, a familiar landmark visible for many miles. Its vast summit is like a small plateau, with three peaks – An Cabar on the south-west corner, Tom a' Choinnich in the north-east and between them the highest top, and thus the Munro, Glas Leathad Mor.

The easiest way to access the hill is from the large Forestry Commission car park, just off the A835 about 8km (5 miles) north of Garve. A great path leads to the hill and the simplest route is an up-and-down from the car park. In good weather it's a very straightforward route, if a little bit of a steep drag on the zig-zags to the first top, An Cabar ("the antler").

Its proximity to Inverness means it's a very popular Munro, with more than 8000 ascents by the normal route each year.

Glas Leathad Mor and much of the rest of Ben Wyvis has been designated a National Nature Reserve, cared for by Scottish National Heritage (SNH). It's also a Special Protection Area.

The summit is covered in moss, rather than the heather or grass you'd perhaps expect on a Scottish hill. It's a delicate environment and one of the largest examples of the habitat in Scotland.

> Pronunciation: *Glass Lehat More (Ben Wiv-is)*; Meaning: big green-grey slope (hill of terror)
> Height: 1046m (3432ft); Rank: 85
> OS Landranger Map 20
> Summit grid ref: NH463684 (trig point & wind shelter)

Overgrazing and erosion from many thousands of boots have taken their toll over the years, and restoration of the moss is a key aim of SNH.

Numbers of grazing animals are controlled and much work has been done to improve paths in the area – there's now an "official", clear path that walkers are encouraged to use. Previously, a multitude of unofficial paths had developed, causing much damage to a delicate ecosystem. Conservation workers have also been transplanting moss to eroded areas.

As Ben Wyvis is an isolated mountain, rising high above its surroundings, views on a clear day from the summit are extensive and impressive – south-east is the Moray Firth, and west lies a great array of peaks.

Despite the hill's popularity and ease of access, it shouldn't be underestimated. Conditions, even in the middle of summer, can be wild. Navigation on the plateau can present a challenge in poor visibility, and

Ben Wyvis from the Black Isle

walkers should always be equipped with the usual map, compass and foul-weather gear.

THE ROUTE

The large Forestry Commission car park 8km (5 miles) north of Garve and on the east side of the A835 is well signposted.

From the north end of the car park, a good path crosses the Allt a' Bhealaich Mhoir via a bridge, and then turns sharp right to follow the river through mature woodland.

As the climb continues, the woodland thins. The gradient eases somewhat and the woods are left behind.

The well-built track leads over easy ground to the start of the climb proper, where it zig-zags steeply up the hillside to An Cabar. It's a bit of a slog in places.

From An Cabar, the summit of Glas Leathad Mor is 2km (1.2 miles) north-east. It's easy walking on the pleasant ground of the wide, mossy ridge.

From the summit, the easiest route of return, and that reflected in the figures above, is simply to retrace your steps.

JAMES ROBERTSON

The first person known to have climbed Ben Nevis, the botanist James Robertson, also made the first recorded ascent of Ben Wyvis.

The Edinburgh academic's journals, held by the National Library of Scotland, record that he climbed the hill in June 1767 – four years before he climbed Ben Nevis.

Robertson had been commissioned to investigate areas of Highlands forfeited in the aftermath of Culloden for botanical and mineralogical potential. Of his summer ascent he wrote: "On the summit I was whitened by a fall of snow, and in many lower parts of the mountain it lay underfoot to a considerable depth."

Robertson also noted that he used a map and compass on the mountain – making him, according to the author Ian R. Mitchell, possibly the first hillwalker with such equipment.

Although his is the first recorded ascent, Ben Wyvis is so prominent and accessible – as well as being very straightforward in good weather – that it's very unlikely Robertson was the first person to climb it.

An alternative is to continue to the third top, Tom a' Choinnich and then descend from that summit by its south-west ridge. You'll pick up a path alongside the Allt a' Gharbh Bhaid and through the forest. After a while, the path meets a forest road – turning right along it will take you back to the path alongside the Allt a' Bhealaich Mhoir which was followed on the inward route.

Did You Know?

As much as 2% of the UK's population of dotterel can be found on Ben Wyvis. Other birdlife includes ptarmigan, snow bunting and golden plover.

Looking towards Ullapool from Ben Wyvis

Mam Sodhail reflected on Loch Beinn a' Mheadhoin

Carn Eighe from Mam Sodhail at sunrise

Did You Know?
Glen Affric contains the third-largest area of native pine woods in Scotland. Some of the Scots pines are estimated to be well over 200 years old.

39
Mam Sodhail

HIDDEN deep down Glen Affric, Mam Sodhail is among a clutch of hard-to-reach Munros – bagging any of the peaks here demands commitment and requires long days.

The "ticks" might be hard-earned but the walking is among some of the most scenic parts of the country. Glen Affric is often described as "Scotland's most beautiful glen" and campaigners have long believed the area should be designated a National Park.

The glen is home to one of the most wonderful examples of native pine forest remaining in Scotland. The woods contain many "granny" pines – ancient, gnarled trees several centuries old.

The blend of Scots pine and rugged mountains rising from the loch-side makes for the quintessential romantic vision of Highland Scotland – all that's needed is a big, antlered stag to set off the scene.

Mam Sodhail, on the north side of the glen, can be climbed as a single Munro – but the Munro of Carn Eige, 1183m (3881ft) lies less than a kilometre from the summit and doesn't involve much up and down. Most walkers will take in both hills.

Keen Munro-baggers often try to include Beinn Fhionnlaidh, 1005m (3297ft) in the round – it lies some 2km (1.2 miles) north of Carn Eige. Treated as

Pronunciation: *Mam So-ail*
Meaning: hill of the barns
Height: 1181m (3875ft); Rank: 14
OS Landranger Map 25
Summit grid ref: NH120253
(enormous hollow cairn)

a there-and-back, this third Munro will add a good couple of hours to the day, but that should be balanced against the fact it's incredibly difficult to reach the hill by any other way. Chartering a boat to take you along Loch Mullardoch and approaching from the north is one option.

The route I recommend takes in the three Munros as a day walk – a long day. It's a slight modification of a route I did with my friend Andy Buchan. We added in the Munros Toll Creagach and Tom a' Choinich, which lie at the eastern end of the glen, before ascending Carn Eige and Beinn Fhionnlaidh.

We camped at the Bealach Beag, at the foot of Beinn Fhionnlaidh, where a short descent east is a source of water. The next morning, we skirted Carn Eige to climb Mam Sodhail, which was particularly memorable for me as it was my 200th Munro.

Whichever route you walk, I recommend including Sgurr na Lapaich,

Mam Sodhail, sunrise

NEAREST TOWN: Cannich is around 23km (14.3 miles) north-east. The village has a post office/shop, a campsite, self-catering options and B&Bs. There's also a pub, The Slaters Arms, where refreshment is well deserved after reaching such a remote hill.

RECOMMENDED ROUTE
Start grid ref: NH216242
Distance: 28km (17.4 miles)
Ascent: 1930m (6332ft)
Time: 11hrs

an official Munro Top of Mam Sodhail. With a separation of around 3.5km (2.2 miles) from the main summit, and reaching 1036m (3399ft) it's a fine peak in its own right – and was once regarded a separate Munro, being deleted from the tables in 1921. Future revisions should, I believe, see it restored.

THE ROUTE

I think it's best to walk this route anticlockwise – the south-east ridge of Sgurr na Lapaich is pretty steep and would be a bit of a slog in ascent. It's a much more gradual climb to Carn Eige.

Approaching from Cannich in the east, there's a large parking area at the end of the public road in Glen Affric.

Follow the track at the road end. It runs on the north side of the burn and soon becomes a path. After around 2km (1.2 miles), a junction is reached – continue on the main track, which now heads west, still on the north of the river, into Gleann nam Fiadh.

After another 2km (1.2 miles), stick to a higher path that climbs away from the river into Coire Mhic Fhearchair. Your aim is the col east of Sron Garbh.

From the bealach, head west on a superb old stalkers' path – which even includes a section resembling a stone staircase.

The narrow ridge leads to Carn Eige

Loch Benevan and Mam Sodhail

and can include some fun scrambling – otherwise there's an easy bypass path.

From the summit, descend the north ridge over Stob Coire Lochan to the Bealach Beag – from there it's little more than 1km (0.6 miles) and a climb of 170m (558ft) to the summit of Beinn Fhionnlaidh.

Retrace your steps but rather than again crossing the summit of Carn Eige, it can instead be skirted on its western flank on a shoulder just beneath the summit.

Make a rising traverse, across a couple of stony sections, to the bealach with Mam Sodhail. From here, a path leads south to the summit. The views are grand – hence its importance to the Ordnance Survey.

A narrow, but easy, ridge descends south-east to a col before Sgurr na Lapaich. A steep pull on by-now-tired legs takes you to the summit. From here, continue to pick your way south-east then, once off the hill, head east across boggy ground to pick up a stalkers' path that takes you out to near Affric Lodge. Then follow the road east and back to the car park.

EARLY SURVEYORS

At 1181m (3875ft) high, Glen Affric's Mam Sodhail is the second-highest mountain in Scotland north of the Great Glen.

It's beaten only by its near neighbour – some say twin – Carn Eige, a Munro just 2m (6ft) taller, less than a kilometre away and separated by a drop of under 150m (492ft).

Mam Sodhail's prominence meant it was an important peak in the early days of the Ordnance Survey's work in Scotland on the "Primary Triangulation" – the measuring of set points in the landscape in relation to one another. It formed the basis of the first OS maps and took place between 1791 and 1853.

In 1848, surveyors spent a month on Mam Sodhail's summit. They built an enormous stone tower 7m (23ft) high. All that remains today is its base, around 2m (6ft) high. It's still an impressive structure. Hollow and rectangular inside, it can be climbed into for shelter.

Summit of Fionn Bheinn

The Eastern Fannaichs

Did You Know?

Seven miles east of Achnasheen is the grave of Scots aviation pioneer Captain Bertram Dickson. He died in 1913 of injuries sustained three years earlier in the world's first mid-air collision.

40
Fionn Bheinn

MOUNTAIN writers tend to be a bit disparaging when it comes to Fionn Bheinn – "undistinguished", "unexciting" and "uninspiring" are some of the rather negative adjectives used.

I think this is unfair. Admittedly, the short ascent is a wade through a bog then a slog up grassy slopes, but the reward is a truly incredible view – easily one of the most stunning in, not just the North-West Highlands, but the whole of Scotland.

Fionn Bheinn can be climbed in four hours in summer conditions – a perfect half-day for those planning a weekend walking in Torridon. After all, you drive through Achnasheen, on the A832, as you head west.

A brief stop off, in clear weather, to ascend Fionn Bheinn will reveal the hills that await in the days to come – it's an awe-inspiring sight.

West, the Torridon giants soar from flat, sea-level plains. There's Liathach, then the grey-white monster of Beinn Eighe and, further north, the unmistakable outline of Slioch. If these are your targets in coming days, it's a sight that's sure to quicken the pulse.

As your eyes continue to trace an arc north they'll find Lochan Fada, before alighting on the jumble of peaks of the

Pronunciation: *Fee-on Ven*
Meaning: white hill
Height: 933m (3061ft); Rank: 245
OS Landranger Maps 20 & 25
Summit grid ref: NH147621 (trig point)

Fisherfield Forest – the most remote of Scotland's Munros.

The 360-degree panorama continues to your north and west where the rest of the Fannaich mountains lie, beyond Loch Fannich.

It's quite a view, and one that reveals itself suddenly, taking you by surprise as you approach the summit from Creagan na Laogh, especially as for the previous hour or so you've been staring at the grass slope in front of you or stumbling through a wet, tussocky marshland.

Leading to Fionn Bheinn's summit is a nice ridge, riven on the north side by two big corries. It's another fine feature, and one totally unsuspected from the roadside at Achnasheen.

Fionn Bheinn has a stunning summit view

THE ROUTE

Head back to the main road from the car park in the centre of Achnasheen.

At the telephone box, take the old road over the bridge and turn right, through a gate on a track that takes you to a water-treatment works.

The traditional path climbs steeply up open hillside on the right bank of the Allt Achadh na Sine. However, on the left bank a service track to a hydro dam further up the river has been bulldozed up the hillside. It's not the prettiest of routes, but the zig-zags make for a very easy ascent.

From the dam, head across very boggy ground to the nose of Creagan an Laogh. From the small cairn here, head north across a dip before climbing to the ridge that leads to Fionn Bheinn's summit just over 1km (0.6 miles) away. The going is much more pleasant than the bog below – mostly on short grass and moss.

Once you've finished admiring the astonishing views, retrace your steps for a few hundred metres before heading south to skirt Creagan na Laogh on the way back to the dam. Then retrace your steps to Achnasheen.

The view west from Fionn Bheinn

THE BRAHAN SEER

The Highland seer – or prophet – Kenneth Mackenzie predicted that: "The day will come when a raven, attired in plaid and bonnet, will drink his fill of human blood on Fionn-bheinn, three times a day, for three successive days."

It hasn't happened … yet.

Mackenzie, the Brahan Seer, was born at the beginning of the 17th century. His gift of second sight was thanks to a blue stone with a hole in its centre, through which he could see the future. It's said to have been given to his mother by the ghost of a Norwegian princess, with the instruction she pass it to her son.

Among events he's said to have foretold are the Clearances, Culloden and the construction of the Caledonian Canal.

Mackenzie was put to death on the orders of Lady Seaforth, who had him burned as a witch in a tar barrel with metal spikes driven through its sides.

THE
CAIRNGORMS

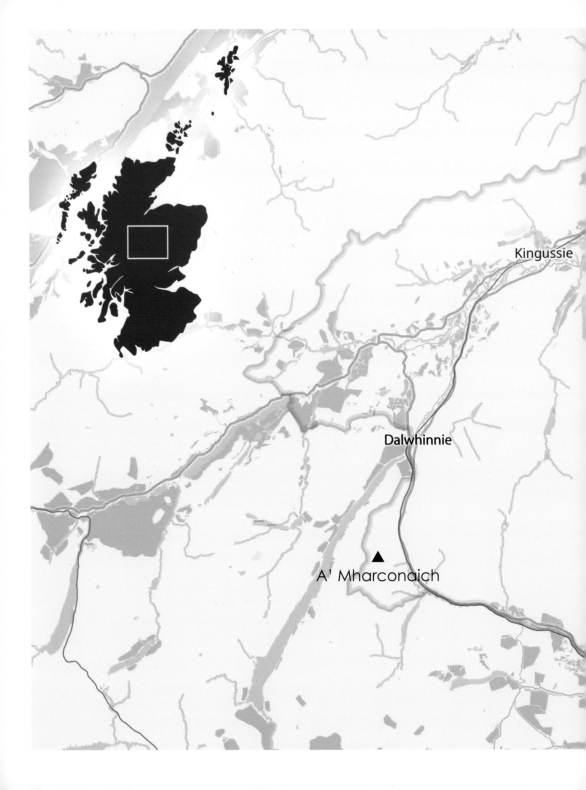

Did You Know?

The Drumochter Pass is the highest point of the rail network, at 452m (1484ft). As well as the railway, the A9 road and Sustrans Cycling Route 7 run through the narrow pass.

41
A' Mharconaich

PART of a tight cluster of four Munros just west of the Drumochter Pass, A' Mharconaich will be a familiar site to anyone travelling to and from the Highlands on the A9.

Pronunciation: *A-var-con-ich*
Meaning: the horse place
Height: 975m (3199ft); Rank: 179
OS Landranger Map 42
Summit grid ref: NN604763 (cairn)

A' Mharconaich is the most distinct of these mountains, its shapely, rolling outline well seen from the roadside.

The Drumochter Munros can have a bit of a bad rep among some hillwalkers. They're often dismissed as "boggy, shapeless lumps", worthy of climbing only because of their Munro status by those ticking off the list.

Sure, they're not dramatic hills. They don't have towering, rocky peaks, and their ascents won't be as exciting as those of certain other hills, but it's still not a fair assessment – they've got their good points.

Their proximity to the roadside gives easy access; the height of your likely start point means much of the hard work is already done; it's a tight-knit group, meaning you can get all four summits in a single trip. Pick the right day and this is a pleasant, high-level moorland yomp with superb views into the Ben Alder range, which you seldom otherwise get the chance to see.

A' Mharconaich is a special hill for me as it was my 141st Munro – the halfway point. I walked the route with my friend Ron Dorn and what made the day even more memorable was that the hill was his 100th Munro – a double celebration!

We walked them in early April, while winter snows still lay and the frozen ground made easy walking of the boggy lower slopes.

In very changeable weather, we walked all four Munros, sometimes enjoying superb views, while at other times howling wind and snow showers reduced visibility to almost zero.

En route to A' Mharconaich, in one of those sudden squally, nasty showers, we met a lone walker stumbling out of the mist just at the cairn of the lower summit of Beinn Udlamain.

We shouted a few words, he took our picture, and then the mist swallowed him once more. We never saw another soul all day.

In full winter conditions, these hills would make a fine ski-touring or snowshoeing expedition.

Glen Truim from A' Mharconaich

RECOMMENDED ROUTE
Start grid ref: NN632755
Distance: 25km (15.5 miles)
Ascent: 1100m (3609ft)
Time: 7hrs

THE ROUTE

I suspect most walkers split these four
Munros into two walks – climbing A'
Mharconaich with Geal Charn, and
Sgairneach Mhor with Beinn Udlamain.

But if you're reasonably fit, and
conditions allow, walking all four in a day is
pretty satisfying. It's a decent day out with
just 1100m (3609ft) of ascent – not bad for
four Munros. Fitter walkers will consider
adding in the Sow of Atholl, a Corbett.

The initial approach, and the walk out,
make use of some of the many tracks that
have been bulldozed up the hillsides in
recent years to allow access for hunting
parties. They're not the prettiest, but they
make for quick going. Using bikes to get

back to the car also saves a lot of time,
which means these hills make for a superb
late-winter/early-spring outing, when, I
believe, they're at their best.

Much of this route is over relatively
featureless plateau, so careful navigation is
needed in poor visibility.

Start by driving to the car park at
Balsporran Cottages (NN628792). Here,
you can leave your bike, chaining it to a
convenient fence. Then drive south for
about 5km (3.1 miles) to layby number 79.

Take the old road from the layby,
through a gate. After a short distance, fork
right on to a track that takes you under the
railway.

After fording a small stream, follow the
Allt Coire Dhomhain on a good track on its
north bank. After about 1.5km (0.9 miles),
ford the river (if safe) and head south-west
on to the long ridge that takes you to the
summit of Sgairneach Mhor. From here,
make for the col at the head of Coire
Dhomhain, then almost directly north for a

Beinn Alder and Loch Ericht

little over 1.5km (0.9 miles) to the summit of Beinn Udlamain, the highest of the four Munros at 1010m (3314ft).

Take in this hill's lower summit and continue roughly north-east across the bealach and on to the summit of A' Mharconaich. You can descend via the long north-east ridge back to Balsporran, or backtrack a few hundred metres before heading north-west to the bealach with Gael Charn, then north for the summit.

The descent from Gael Charn can be a bit of a plod in deep, tussocky heather until you pick up another of the bulldozed tracks that take you back to Balsporran, where the waiting bikes are a welcome sight.

The cycle path along the A9 makes for a speedy return to your vehicle – although my friend Ron gloomily insists that the quite flat route is entirely uphill!

THE BOAR AND THE SOW

The two hills closest to the road and guarding the western approach to our route are known as the Boar of Badenoch and the Sow of Atholl.

The southern hill, the Sow, is a Corbett at 803m (2635ft). The Gaelic name of its northern neighbour is An Torc, The Boar, and it is indeed in the district of Badenoch – so its English translation is accurate.

Scottish hill legend Hamish Brown reckons the Sow's name is much more recent and fanciful however. In his *Climbing the Corbetts*, he says it's probably a fairly recent invention, given to balance its partner. The hill's original name is Meall an Dobhrachan, or Watercress Hill.

Dawn seen from A' Mharconaich

> ### Did You Know?
> Glen Shee means "the fairy glen" and its Cairnwell Pass lies at 670m (2198ft), making for short ascents of many of the hills in this area.

View to An Socach's eastern summit

42
An Socach (Glen Ey)

AS a wee rounded hill surrounded by big rounded hills, An Socach is a Munro that is often overlooked by hillwalkers – literally as well as figuratively.

It's very close to the Glenshee ski centre, and this wonderful little hill offers a great escape from the skiing infrastructure that, frankly, scars so much of the landscape around here.

Taken as a single Munro, it's not a big walk – either in terms of distance or ascent. This makes it an excellent hill for the short days of winter.

Approached from the north-east, it's a long whaleback to the first top, then a lovely 2km (1.2 mile) walk along a broad ridge to the summit. It's rather a gradual ascent, with a short, steep slope to the first summit. This makes An Socach a great snowshoe outing.

On old maps, the east top is marked as the summit – and the large cairn and wind shelter here probably catch out some baggers.

The true, western, summit is also marked by a wind shelter. Shortly beyond this is a small cairn and from here the highlight of an ascent of An Socach is best appreciated – the incredible view.

In winter especially, with snow coating the land, the sheer majesty of the Cairngorm plateau to the north-west

Pronunciation: *An-sok-cach*
Meaning: the snout, or beak
Height: 944m (3097ft); Rank: 227
OS Landranger Map 43
Summit grid ref: NO080800 (cairn)

is revealed. From Beinn Bhrotain and Braeriach in the north-west, the savage cleft of the Lairig Ghru, then, hunched above all, the great rounded shoulders of Ben Macdui. The Munro of Devil's Point is also easily picked out, looking tiny surrounded by such giants. I reckon it's one of the best viewpoints for the southern aspect of the plateau you'll find.

Ascending the eastern summit

Although popular, the hills around An Socach can still feel empty

NEAREST TOWN: Braemar is 10km (6.2 miles) north. A popular tourist town with a variety of accommodation, shops and amenities to suit all budgets. It also holds the record for the lowest temperature recorded in the UK, -27.2°C.

RECOMMENDED ROUTE
Start grid ref: NO139832
Distance: 16km (9.9 miles)
Ascent: 650m (2133ft)
Time: 5hrs

THE ROUTE

This route avoids all the infrastructure of Glenshee ski centre – from where this hill can also be climbed. It makes for a quieter, much more pleasant walk.

Start point is 6km (3.7 miles) north of the Cairnwell Pass and ski centre on the A93 Braemar Road. A track leaves the road on the left for Baddoch Farm – there's limited room here for a few vehicles. Be careful not to block access. If parking's not possible, there's a large layby a few hundred metres south.

Head along the farm track – there might be some friendly horses here to greet you.

Once past the farm buildings, follow the Land Rover track along the south bank of the Baddoch Burn. The track crosses the burn after about 1km (0.6 miles). Roughly another 1km (0.6 miles) further on, you ford the Allt Coire Fhearneasg.

Immediately after crossing this stream, strike off up the hill, initially following the river for a short distance before heading south-east along the ridge.

After reaching a massive cairn, traverse a boggier, flatter section before a steep pull, then rockier ground to the east summit. From here, it's a pleasant high-level traverse on a broad ridge to the true summit some 2km (1.2 miles) west.

After savouring the stunning views, simply retrace your steps.

The road to Baddoch Farm and the start of the route

The track crosses several fords

THE DEVIL'S ELBOW

The A93 road north from the Spittal of Glenshee up over the Cairnwell Pass to the start of our route includes a long, very steep section known as the "Devil's Elbow" – even though it's quite straight. The name is also used on many maps, and it's how locals usually refer to the stretch.

This is because the road to the ski centre is relatively modern – the "old road", before the 1970s, was a notoriously twisty and steep single track.

The section known as the Devil's Elbow included two nightmarish hairpin bends and had a gradient of 1 in 6 (17%). It was so steep, buses stopped at the bottom and passengers had to walk up. The AA also stocked an emergency layby to help drivers with overheating engines.

Parts of the old road can still be seen in sections next to the modern route.

Ben Macdui summit

Did You Know?

The first recorded ascent of Ben Macdui was in 1810, by Reverend Dr George Keith, who measured the height of the hill and angered locals.

Ben Macdui from Derry Cairngorm

43
Ben Macdui

IT'S Scotland's second-highest mountain, but Ben Macdui was once believed to be the highest.

When it was discovered in the early 19th century that Ben Nevis was almost 40m (131ft) higher, locals were distraught.

They clubbed together, determined to build a giant cairn to claim the number-one spot. Fortunately, their lofty plans were never carried out.

Ben Macdui remains, however, a mighty mountain. It forms the steep eastern wall of the Lairig Ghru, the great cleft that slices through the Cairngorms.

The mountain, together with its neighbour Cairn Gorm, forms the vast area known as the Cairngorm plateau – the largest area of sub-arctic terrain in the UK, with more than 20km² (7.7 miles sq.) above 1000m (3281ft).

In the mid 19th century, Ordnance Survey built an observatory near the summit. The remains of the drystone buildings can be seen there today. They're roofless but the tumbledown walls can provide welcome shelter from the wild weather that often batters the summit.

Near the huge summit cairn is a view indicator, constructed in 1925 by members of Aberdeen's Cairngorm Club, in memory of Alexander Copland, a past president of the club.

Pronunciation: *Ben Mack-doo-ay*
Meaning: MacDuff's hill
Height: 1309m (4295ft); Rank: 2
OS Landranger Maps 36 & 43
Summit grid ref: NN989989 (large cairn & trig point)

The first time I climbed Ben Macdui was on midsummer's day a number of years ago. Although quite pleasant in the glens, the tops were covered in thick clag. There was ice underfoot on the summit plateau, while wind-driven snow and sleet stung us through our clothing, as if we were being pelted by little stones – it was more like midwinter.

When I climbed the hill with photographer Keith Fergus, on the day he took the images on these pages, conditions couldn't have been more different. It was September and the sun blazed from the sky from dawn until dusk.

Ben Macdui can be linked with several other Munros in the area, in a variety of combinations. It makes for big days over long distances, but the walking is generally quite easy on excellent tracks and paths. Keith and I took advantage of the perfect conditions on our outing and included Beinn Mheadhoin and Cairn Gorm in our round.

NEAREST TOWN: Aviemore is about 20km (12.4 miles) to the north-west. A bustling town in the heart of the Cairngorms, it has a railway station, a wide variety of accommodation, bars and restaurants, and several equipment shops.

RECOMMENDED ROUTE
Start grid ref: NH989061
Distance: 15km (9.3 miles)
Ascent: 800m (2625ft)
Time: 6hrs

THE ROUTE

Sitting at the heart of the Cairngorm plateau, there are several ways to reach Ben Macdui, and the hill can be climbed in combination with a variety of other Munros.

The route I recommend here is the easiest – a simple there-and-back from the ski centre. The route has the advantage that the start point sits at about 600m (1968ft) above sea level, and it can easily be altered to include other summits, depending on fitness and weather conditions.

A well-constructed path leads south-west from the ski-centre base station. At a junction after 500m (1640ft), take the lower, right-hand fork. A short distance further on is another junction – again take the right-hand path.

After crossing the burn that flows from Coire an Lochain, head for the middle of the wide ridge of Miadan Creag an Leth-choin.

A track takes you near Pt 1083, from which it's an easy 3.5km (2.2 mile) walk just east of south to the summit. The ground rises gently and the path fades in stony ground, but it's a straightforward walk in good weather.

The view indicator points out the highlights. Just across the Lairig Ghru, Cairn Toul and Braeriach are particularly impressive, with deep corries scooped from their flanks.

Cloud inversion seen from Ben Macdui

Simply retrace your steps for the return.

Other options include leaving the return path after a couple of kilometres for another path that skirts Lochan Buidhe – it takes you to the cliffs above Coire an t-Sneachda, from where it's easy to include Cairn Gorm, using the route described elsewhere in these pages.

Alternatively, heading south-east then east from the summit – past the observatory ruins – takes you on a path to Loch Etchachan. From this path, Derry Cairngorm can easily be climbed, or Beinn Mheadhoin from the loch-side.

In good summer weather, these routes give pleasant walking on good tracks. But the plateau can be a wild, dangerous place – not just in winter. There have been many tragic deaths in these hills.

THE BIG GREY MAN

A supernatural presence is said to stalk the slopes of Ben Macdui – Am Fear Liath Mor, or The Big Grey Man.

James Hogg, the poet known as the Ettrick Shepherd, referred to the presence in verses as far back as 1791, but it was in 1925 that it came to prominence.

It was then that renowned climber Professor J. Norman Collie, related his encounter with The Big Grey Man more than 30 years previously in 1891.

He described being seized by a feeling of terror and panic while on the mountain, and hearing a giant's footsteps shadow his own.

Most encounters detail this feeling of fear and unease, rather than a physical sighting. However, in 1958, a report by mountaineer Alexander Tewnion was published in *The Scots Magazine*. He described being charged at by a large figure looming from the mist while climbing Ben Macdui during leave from the RAF in 1943. He shot at the figure three times with his revolver.

The path to Ben Macdui

Loch Eanaich from Sgor Gaoith

Sgoran Dubh Mor from Sgor Gaoith

Did You Know?

A short distance north of Sgor Gaoith lies another peak, Sgoran Dubh Mor. The 1111m (3645ft) hill was once also a Munro but lost that status as it was deemed too close to the higher summit.

44
Sgor Gaoith

IF you had just one day to spend exploring the Cairngorms, you could do no better than a walk along Glen Feshie, taking in Sgor Gaoith and its neighbouring Munro Mullach Clach a' Bhlair.

In a single day out, this route encapsulates the incredible variety of landscape, climate, animal and plant life that makes this part of Scotland so special.

The usual start and finish point for walks here is at Achlean – just a half-hour drive on mostly single-track roads from Aviemore. It feels much more remote though – far from the bustle of the tourist industry centred around the Highland town and the nearby Cairn Gorm mountain.

Your journey takes you up one of the most beautiful glens in the country, on excellent tracks on the valley floor beside the cool waters of the River Feshie.

Later, you climb among mighty Scots pines – some easily 300 years old – as the path twists among sections of native woodland. Underfoot, either side of the track, are thick carpets of blueberry, heather and wildflowers.

The area bursts with life – butterflies and bees flit between flowers, and the woodlands are a stronghold of the red squirrel, a creature under so much pressure elsewhere.

Later, as you climb into the mountains,

Pronunciation: *S-gaw-r Goo-ay*
Meaning: peak of the wind
Height: 1118m (3668ft); Rank: 37
OS Landranger Maps 36 & 43
Summit grid ref: NN903989 (cairn)

you reach the Moine Mhor – or Great Moss – an enormous shallow bowl 1000m (3281ft) above the valley and home to the two Munros.

It's lower than the vast plateau of the Cairngorm hills, which sits just to the east over Glen Einich, and I think it's also more attractive. In high summer it's a verdant, almost lush place – at least as far as high mountains are concerned.

Mullach Clach a' Bhlair is just a slight rise on this vast plain – unless they're Munro-baggers most probably don't bother walking to it. But it makes a great start point for a fantastic high-level moorland walk of more than 6km (3.7 miles) to Sgor Gaoith.

West lie the wonderfully bleak lands of the Monadh Liath, but it's the east that draws the eye. It's from the small summit of Sgor Gaoith that you get the best view – the ground drops in a vertical plunge to the gorgeous waters of Loch Einich. The huge bulk of Braeriach across the glen

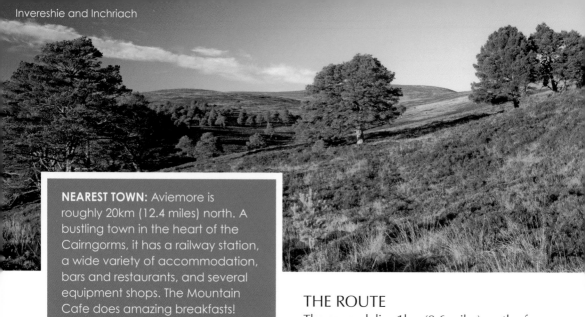

looks close enough to touch, its corries great gouges in its western flanks. It's a rare view of one of the highest mountains in the country – indeed, it must rank as one of the best views in Scotland.

With winter snows, this land is transformed into an Arctic wilderness. Storms can rise with a sudden ferocity, reducing visibility to zero, winds so severe that standing, never mind walking, is impossible.

And yet, on good days, the enormous snowy bowl makes a fantastic winter playground. Ski-touring or – as I tend to do – snowshoeing between the peaks makes for a memorable expedition.

THE ROUTE

The car park lies 1km (0.6 miles) north of the road end at Achlean.

Follow the road south then take a signed track to avoid the farmhouse. Continue along the east bank of the River Feshie.

There are a couple of streams and rivers to ford on this section, which could prove tricky – or even impossible – after heavy rains.

The excellent path leads you through birch woods, then mature pinewoods full of impressive Scots pines.

Eventually you'll reach a crossroad of tracks – take the left branch. The bulldozed route rises up into Coire Caol and all the way on to the plateau. At the bealach, there's a junction – the right-hand fork leads almost all the way to the summit of Mullach a' Clach Bhlair.

The tracks are quite unsightly – something of a scar on what otherwise feels like remote, wild land. They do make for quick progress however.

From this summit, head just east of north to Carn Ban Mor. From there it's less than 2km (1.2 miles) north-east to the summit of Sgor Gaoith with its wonderful views.

The return route sees you head back to Carn Ban Mor. Rather than take in the summit again, skirt it on the north-west flank to pick up a track – the Foxhunter's Path – that takes you down into Coire Fhearnagan and out to Achlean.

In summer and winter this can be a pleasant walk – although the Moine Mor can be a bit soggy when there's no snow cover. In poor visibility, the relatively featureless plateau presents a very difficult navigational challenge. The great cliffs on which Sgor Gaoith's summit cairn perches are also prone to cornice in winter. Great care is needed.

A REWILDED GLEN

Glenfeshie Estate is owned by reclusive Danish billionaire Anders Holch Povlsen.

Povlsen – who owns several Highland estates – is now the second-largest individual landowner in the UK and the largest shareholder at online fashion retailer ASOS.

Since 2006, a programme of rewilding has been carried out on his Glen Feshie lands. Part of this involved a heavy reduction of deer numbers to allow the regeneration of woodland.

The cull was controversial as it included stalking – but not shooting – by helicopter and taking deer out of season.

But, with deer having no natural predators since the extinction of wolves and lynx in Scotland and numbers getting out of control, it was argued such drastic action was needed to bring balance to the ecosystem.

Today, the glen is rapidly regenerating and is already a land transformed from its recent past as an overgrazed, ecologically impoverished deer forest.

Looking over to the Southern Cairngorms

Cairn Gorm from the Northern Corries

Cairn Gorm

Did You Know?

At 1097m (3599ft), the Ptarmigan Restaurant – housed in the funicular railway's top station – is the highest in the UK. It's the perfect place to call in for a hot chocolate when descending Cairn Gorm.

45
Cairn Gorm

THE sixth-highest mountain in the UK and home to one of our premier ski resorts, Cairn Gorm is a busy mountain.

It has an enormous summit cairn and, somewhat unusually, a weather station providing forecasts for the thousands of skiers who visit annually.

The skiing infrastructure can be unsightly – especially in summer when it sits idle and has a kind of post-industrial feel. That said, the road into Coire Cas and the base station make accessing the hills here very easy.

The mountain is also home to Scotland's only funicular railway. In summer it operates as a closed-loop system – those who take it to the top station a couple of hundred metres below the summit are no longer allowed to access the open hill. This has drastically reduced summer footfall on the plateau. Countless thousands of feet that made that short journey previously left a wide, eroded scar on the land.

With the reduction in numbers, the area is recovering – slowly. At such altitude and in poor soils, vegetation will take many decades to be fully restored.

Despite not being the highest mountain in the area – that honour goes to nearby Ben Macdui – Cairn Gorm has given its

Pronunciation: *Care-n Gawrm*
Meaning: blue hill
Height: 1245m (4085ft); Rank: 6
OS Landranger Map 36
Summit grid ref: NJ005040 (large cairn, mast and weather station)

name to the entire range of hills. While the infrastructure and crowds make this hill feel far from remote, the views from the summit are wonderful – laid before you is the vast expanse of the plateau. It's a unique and precious landscape – the UK's only sub-arctic environment.

Other than Ben Nevis, there is no land higher in the UK than the Cairngorms. The massif is exposed to the full force of storms blowing in from the west, with nothing to break their fury. The plateau is often windswept and wild – not a place to linger. Winter months can be particularly ferocious, with white-outs lasting days common.

The mountain is a favourite with winter and summer rock climbers. Good days will see dozens of teams on the faces of the Northern Corries. The extreme conditions mean it's also the ideal place for walkers and climbers to learn winter skills. You'll often find large parties of students digging snow holes or practising ice-axe arrests.

NEAREST TOWN: Aviemore town centre is about 14km (8.8 miles) north-west of the summit. A bustling town in the heart of the Cairngorms, it has a railway station, a wide variety of accommodation, bars and restaurants, and several equipment shops. Cairngorm Brewery makes for a refreshing pit stop!

RECOMMENDED ROUTE
Start grid ref: NH989061
Distance: 11km (6.8 miles)
Ascent: 775m (2543ft)
Time: 5hrs

THE ROUTE

Despite plenty of winter days climbing in the Northern Corries, I've only been to Cairn Gorm summit twice, usually descending instead via the Goat Track or Fiacaill a' Choire Chais from Pt 1140m – from where a detour 500m (1640ft) east and a climb of 100m (328ft) would take you to the Munro summit. Coire an t-Sneachda has several low-grade climbs and easy gullies that would make this a fun option for parties with appropriate climbing skills and equipment.

There are many options for walkers on Cairn Gorm, and the hill can be linked with several others for long days out. As a single ascent, I'd recommend following the Ben Macdui path from the ski centre base station as far as Coire an Lochain. Then ascend the wide ridge of Maidan Creag an Leth-choin. Keep well right of the crags of the Northern Corries – especially in poor visibility – but follow their line to Cairn Lochan. Continuing along the clifftops for another 2km (1.2 miles) takes you to Pt 1140m as described above. From the summit descend north to the Ptarmigan Restaurant, then follow the ridge back down to the base station.

A more interesting ascent, for those with some scrambling experience, is the

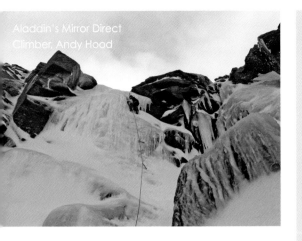
Aladdin's Mirror Direct
Climber, Andy Hood

Fiacaill Ridge. In summer it's a Grade 1 scramble, so you should be comfortable with exposure and competent with your hands on rock. The start point is the same as above but leave the path sooner, heading for the ridge after 1km (0.6 miles) or so. All major difficulties on the route can be bypassed to the right, on easier – but still steep – ground. It'll bring you out on the plateau on the original route, several hundred metres north-east of Cairn Lochan.

Beinn Mheadhoin from Cairn Gorm

A UNIQUE REINDEER HERD

As a unique mountain environment, it's only right Cairn Gorm has a unique resident – the UK's only free-roaming reindeer herd.

Summer or winter, climbers and walkers will find these beautiful beasts on the hillside. Incredibly docile and tame, they're perfectly comfortable around humans – and they'll think nothing of having a snuffle round your pack to check if you've anything to eat, so keep all human food out of reach.

If you don't bump into them on the hill, pay a visit to Cairngorm Reindeer Centre at Glenmore. The reindeer not out roaming spend their time chilling in the 486-hectare (1200-acre) enclosure.

Indigenous to Scotland, reindeer died out sometime after the last Ice Age – possibly because of climate change, or simply overhunting. They were reintroduced in the 1950s by Mikel Utsi and Ethel Lindgren, a married couple with experience of reindeer herding in their native Sweden.

Did You Know?

A wind speed of 283 kph (176 mph) was measured on Cairn Gorm summit on January 3, 1993. It's the highest ever recorded in the UK.

The Northern Corries

The Bynack More path

Bynack More

Did You Know?
The giant granite tors found on the summit of Bynack More are known as the Barns of Bynack.

46

Bynack More

A RELATIVELY lonely hill at the north-eastern corner of the main Cairngorm plateau, Bynack More is separated from its neighbouring Munros by Strath Nethy and upper Glen Avon.

It's a fine, large hill. Its top is an expansive plateau, like many other of the Cairngorm hills. Its actual summit is a cairn among large boulders.

South of the summit there are enormous granite tors, the size of buildings, that burst from the otherwise featureless plateau. These are the Barns of Bynack and are worth a short detour for a closer look. Nearby are smaller tors, the Little Barns of Bynack.

Probably the best view of the hill is from the Strathspey side, from the north. From this aspect, Bynack More appears as a graceful, conical peak, quite apart and distinct from the rounded, hulking giant of Cairn Gorm slightly to the west.

The usual route of ascent starts from just before Glenmore Lodge. The big advantage of this route is you could cycle the first 4km (2.5 miles) or so, to as far as Bynack Stables – which aren't as grand as they sound. All you'll find is a rough shack. Leaving your bike here means, obviously, returning by the same route.

The round trip is roughly 22km (13.7 miles), with 750m (2461ft) of ascent and

> Pronunciation: *Bin-ack More*
> Meaning: big cap
> Height: 1090m (3576ft); Rank: 54
> OS Landranger Map 36
> Summit grid ref: NJ042063 (cairn)

should take about six hours – less if you cycle.

The other highlight of this route is that the start takes you through a nature reserve, with lovely native woodland of birch and ancient Scots pine. It skirts the beautiful An Lochan Uaine before arriving at Ryvoan bothy, meaning an evening walk-in to sleep over and an early ascent are an option. Being so easily accessible, however, means the small bothy is also very popular. It consists of a single room, with a platform that could sleep four. You should be prepared to camp.

Despite all these attractions, I think a better route is a complete traverse of the hill. It's shorter in distance but a tougher route, with considerably more ascent. However, it gives you the full character of the mountain, taking in the Barns, before continuing on to Loch Avon, in the heart of the Cairngorms.

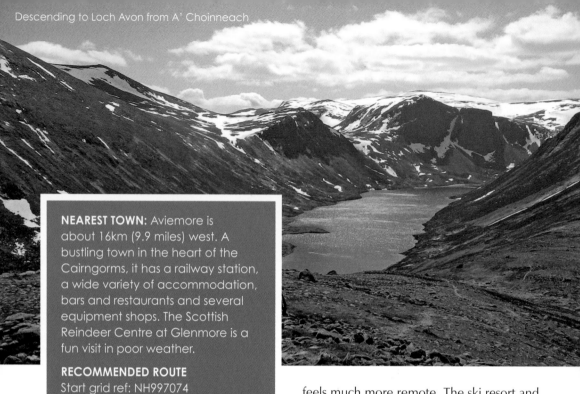

NEAREST TOWN: Aviemore is about 16km (9.9 miles) west. A bustling town in the heart of the Cairngorms, it has a railway station, a wide variety of accommodation, bars and restaurants and several equipment shops. The Scottish Reindeer Centre at Glenmore is a fun visit in poor weather.

RECOMMENDED ROUTE
Start grid ref: NH997074
Distance: 15km (9.3 miles)
Ascent: 1250m (4101ft)
Time: 7hrs

THE ROUTE

Start from the Coire na Ciste car park, picking up a path at its eastern end where the old skiing buildings lie.

A path leads to a small lochan, but you want to stay higher. Make for the col just south of Stac na h-Iolaire – the "rock of the eagle" – marked as Pt 737 on some maps. It's a rising traverse of 1.5km (0.9 miles) through deep heather.

From there, it's a case of picking your way down steep ground to the riverside in Strath Nethy. Although you've not travelled far from the car park, suddenly the area feels much more remote. The ski resort and crowds seem a world away.

Crossing the river is simple when the water's low – you should get across with dry boots. On the far bank, strike up the north-east ridge of Bynack Beg. It's steep at first, again through heather, but you will pick up a path, and the terrain eases higher up.

From Bynack Beg, head south-east for the Munro summit, initially dropping 20m (66ft), before climbing 140m (459ft). It's not hugely steep, but the way is rocky and littered with big boulders.

In nice weather, the Barns are clearly seen – they lie less than 1km (0.6 miles) south-east and are worth a detour.

South-west from the Barns is the summit of A' Choinneach, which you'll

An Lochan Uaine

traverse. It was once a Munro, but was deleted during the 1981 table revision. From the shallow col, it's only an 80m (263ft) ascent.

A path takes you from the summit and winds across stony ground down to the Saddle, at the head of Strath Nethy.

Head north-west from the Saddle, up the broad flanks between Cairn Gorm and Cnap Coire na Spreidhe, heading for Pt 1135. From here, you can head down Sron an Aonaich, between the Ptarmigan Restaurant and the left bank of the Allt na Ciste. It's not the prettiest way out as you follow the line of the old chairlifts, but it takes you directly back to the car park.

The Ryvoan bothy

THE LITTLE GREEN LOCH

Perhaps the most popular route to Bynack More takes you past the stunning An Lochan Uaine – the Little Green Loch.

It's aptly named, as the waters are indeed of a striking green hue. The colour varies with the light – on clear, sunny days it can be a deep, vibrant green. On others, a murky green-blue.

The small loch is less than 2km (1.2 miles) along the track from Glenmore Lodge. I've never read a definitive explanation for its colour – some sources ascribe it to the mineral content of the water, others say it's something to do with the rich undergrowth and impressive mature Scots pine that crowd the shoreline, right to the water's edge.

My favourite explanation comes from local legend – the water is stained green because the fairies, the "wee folk", wash their clothes in it!

Derry Cairngorm from Beinn Mheadhoin

© STEVEN FALLON

Carn Crom from Derry Cairngorm

47
Derry Cairngorm

ANY day involving an ascent of Derry Cairngorm is going to be a long one.

The shortest approach is from Linn of Dee, the first 5km (3.1 miles), and therefore last, of which can be cycled, as far as Derry Lodge. Using a bike – and the track is excellent the whole way – will take hours off your day. It's a no-brainer.

Given it's such a hard hill to reach, most walkers will seek to take maximum advantage of all that effort and bag one, two or even more Munros along with Derry Cairngorm.

The hill's position gives lots of scope for this. A popular combination is to include Ben Macdui – the hills are linked by a very high bealach near Loch Etchachan. Climbing it with Beinn Mheadhoin is another common combination. All three can even be climbed together.

Some will add Carn a' Mhaim, the Munro immediately south of Ben Macdui, to make a trio – or a foursome with Beinn Mheadhoin if you're feeling fit.

A particularly long day that sticks in my mind is when, with a couple of friends, I climbed Beinn Bhreac from Derry Lodge, then Beinn a' Chaorainn and Beinn Mheadhoin before finally traversing Derry Cairngorm and descending back to the Lodge. And yes – we used bikes.

> Pronunciation: *Der-ray Care-n-gawrm*
> Meaning: blue hill of Glen Derry
> Height: 1155m (3789ft); Rank: 20
> OS Landranger Maps 36 & 43
> Summit grid ref: NO017980 (cairn)

All these routes have their attractions, so, with such seemingly endless combinations, I've opted for a simpler approach for my recommended route – climbing it as a single by a pleasing circular route. It can easily be adapted to add in any of the other hills.

The summit of Derry Cairngorm is a massive boulder field – it must be the stoniest of all the Cairngorms' Munros. For 1km (0.6 miles) or so over the summit going can be quite slow as you jump from one giant stone to another. Care is needed as it'd be very easy to turn an ankle, or worse.

Derry Cairngorm is perhaps not the most exciting or sought-after summit in the area, but it is an excellent viewpoint. In fact, it's potentially the best spot for viewing Ben Macdui – the great cliffs that bar the south-west of the UK's second-highest peak look particularly impressive from Derry Cairngorm, as does the secretive Lochan Uaine below them.

NEAREST TOWN: Braemar is 15km (9.3 miles) east. A popular tourist town with a variety of accommodation, shops and amenities to suit all budgets. Balmoral Castle, the Queen's summer home, is just 14.5km (9 miles) away.

RECOMMENDED ROUTE
Start grid ref: NO063897
Distance: 27.5km (17.1 miles)
Ascent: 1100m (3609ft)
Time: 9hrs

THE ROUTE

The approach is via Glen Derry – and a push bike is a great help for roughly the first 5km (3.1 miles) to Derry Lodge.

From the usually very busy Linn of Dee car park (charge) head north on an excellent path through the forest. Turn left on reaching a Land Rover track and follow it to the bridge over Lui Water. Then turn left on to another excellent vehicle track,

which continues to Derry Lodge – this is where you leave your bike if cycling.

A path leads north through native pine forest into Glen Derry, up the east bank of the river. There are a few streams to ford, which can present serious difficulties – or even be impossible to cross – in times of spate. Keep left at a junction and then, after about 0.5km (0.3 miles), cross the river on a bridge.

The track passes the Hutchison Memorial Hut and climbs to Little Loch Etchachan. At a junction follow the left fork. The track climbs easily and steadily south-west on its way to Ben Macdui. Leave the path after about 600m (1968ft), climbing to the west of Creagan a' Choire Etchachan. After reaching a flatter area, the ground drops slightly before beginning to climb to the stony summit of Derry Cairngorm.

Head south-east from the summit, past a cairn on a small rise about 1km (0.6 miles) away. Almost directly south is Carn Crom. Keep to the left of this top, between the summit of the cliffs that fall steeply into Glen Derry.

Continuing south-east takes you over Creag Bad an t-Seabhaig. A path winds its way down into the lovely forest of ancient Scots pine and back to Derry Lodge.

If you've left a bike here, it'll be a welcome sight and an easy coast back to Linn of Dee. If not, it's a 5km (3.1 mile) slog on hard tracks.

Forest of Mar from Derry Cairngorm

THE FIRST ASCENT

The first recorded ascent of Derry Cairngorm happened entirely by accident in 1830!

It was then that a party led by renowned naturalist William MacGillivray traversed the hill after climbing Ben Macdui. They found themselves lost in thick mist and opted to continue over the summit rather than attempt to descend dangerous rocky slopes in poor visibility.

MacGillivray (1796–1852) found fame as "Scotland's greatest field naturalist" and had a particular interest in ornithology.

He was born in Aberdeen but raised by an uncle on the isle of Harris. At just 12, he returned to Aberdeen to study at the university.

During his student years, each summer he would walk west from Aberdeen right across the country to catch a ferry to Harris to spend the holidays.

Before becoming Professor of Natural History at Aberdeen's Marischal College, MacGillivray was curator of the Museum of the Royal College of Surgeons in Edinburgh.

Loch Avon to Beinn Mheadhoin

Beinn Mheadhoin from Coire Domhain

Did You Know?

Sitting above Munro height at an altitude of 927m (3041ft), Loch Etchachan is widely regarded as the highest "proper" loch in Scotland.

48

Beinn Mheadhoin

ANOTHER of Scotland's "middle hills". What sets this one apart, however, is its great height – Beinn Mheadhoin is the 13th-highest Munro – and its incredible remoteness.

It sits in the heart of the Cairngorm massif and just reaching the mountain is quite a challenge. Surrounded by several other of the Cairngorm giants, Beinn Mheadhoin can be climbed in various combinations with its neighbours.

The route I recommend here takes it in as a single Munro, ideally with the help of a bike. But, however you approach the hill, it will involve a long day with much distance and ascent.

Your reward, to experience one of Scotland's most unusual summits – the plateau is littered with a number of giant tors. These enormous granite boulders are relics of the ice age, left behind by the retreating ice. Millennia of subsequent Cairngorm winters and ferocious storms have carved out the lines of weakness in the mighty tors, creating the most wonderful shapes.

Underfoot, the surface consists of tiny granules of granite, like coarse sand. It gives the plateau a strange, Martian feel.

The actual summit is the tallest of these tors, a huge lump that looks impregnable when approached from the south and

> Pronunciation: *Ben Vay-ann*
> Meaning: middle hill
> Height: 1182m (3878ft); Rank: 13
> OS Landranger Map 36
> Summit grid ref: NJ024017 (large granite tor)

west, although it's a fairly easy scramble up the other side.

The best day I had on Beinn Mheadhoin was with Keith Fergus, when he took the pictures used in this chapter. It was in September 2015 – a perfect early-autumn day with warm sun and blue skies.

From the Coire Cas car park, we combined it with an ascent of Ben Macdui and Cairn Gorm, with Beinn Mheadhoin coming, appropriately enough, in the middle.

Loch Avon from Beinn Mheadhoin

NEAREST TOWN: Aviemore is roughly 17km (10.6 miles) west. A bustling town in the heart of the Cairngorms, it has a railway station, a wide variety of accommodation, bars and restaurants, and several equipment shops. Just off the A9, it's well served by buses.

RECOMMENDED ROUTE
Start grid ref: NO063897
Distance: 31km (19.3 miles)
Ascent: 1000m (3281ft)
Time: 10hrs (without a bike)

THE ROUTE

The only way to approach Beinn Mheadhoin without first climbing other hills is by heading up Glen Derry – and a push bike is a great help for the first 5km (3.1 miles) or so.

From the Linn of Dee car park (charge) head north on a great path through the forest. Turn left when you reach a Land Rover track – and then left again after crossing a bridge over Lui Water. Continue to Derry Lodge, where you can leave your bike if cycling.

A path leads north into Glen Derry, following the east bank of the river. There are several streams and rivers to ford, which can present serious difficulties in times of spate. Keep left at a junction before crossing the river on a bridge after about 0.5km (0.3 miles).

The track passes the Hutchison Memorial Hut and climbs to Little Loch Etchachan. An eroded, rocky path winds north-east up Beinn Mheadhoin. The plateau is littered with the granite tors for

THE "HUTCHY HUT"

The route takes you past the Hutchison Memorial Hut – known to generations of climbers as simply the "Hutchy Hut".

Now maintained by the Mountain Bothies Association, it was built in 1954 in memory of Aberdeen climber Dr Arthur Gilbertson Hutchison, who died in a climbing accident in Wales in 1949.

Construction was organised by his friends and it was sited among the hills he loved as a boy. Its purpose was as a mountain refuge, or as somewhere climbers could spend the night.

For much of its existence it was a cold, dank, damp hut with a bare-earth floor.

However, the MBA undertook extensive work on the hut in 2012. It now has a double-glazed window, wooden floor, storm porch, multi-fuel stove and a sleeping platform. Altogether quite luxurious for a bothy!

which the hill is famous. They're worth a visit, involving the shortest detours. The largest tor – the summit – is at the north-east end of the plateau and is reached by a short scramble up its far side. It's an unusual and somehow very satisfying summit. Unless you plan to take in other peaks, the simplest return is to retrace your steps.

Did You Know?

Derry Lodge was a 19th-century shooting lodge and was used by Queen Victoria. The estate is now owned by the National Trust for Scotland.

Lochnagar from Meikle Pap

Did You Know?

Spring water that issues from the Lochnagar hills is used by a local distillery to produce a single malt whisky called Royal Lochnagar. The distillery dates to 1826 and is now owned by drinks giant Diageo.

Loch Muick

49
Lochnagar

F EW Scottish mountains are as famous as Lochnagar, immortalised in verse as 'Dark Lochnagar' by Lord Byron – presumably because the precipitous cliffs of its vast northern corrie rarely see sun, even in summer.

Pronunciation: *Loch-nah-gar*
Meaning: little loch of laughter
Height: 1155m (3789ft); Rank: 21
OS Landranger Map 44
Summit grid ref: NO244861 (trig point on granite tor)

The mountain lies entirely within the Royal Family's Balmoral Estate in the Southern Cairngorms, which was purchased by Queen Victoria and Prince Albert in 1852, having been leased since 1848.

The Royal Family continue to holiday at Balmoral every summer, and Lochnagar is said to be Prince Charles' favourite mountain. He famously wrote the kids' book *The Old Man of Lochnagar*, based on a tale he made up to entertain his younger brothers when they were children, and a print of one of his paintings of the mountain raised thousands at a wildlife charity auction in 2017.

It's also not unknown for hillwalkers to meet the Prince on the hill when the Royals are in residence.

The great sweep of cliffs of Lochnagar's northern corrie are a popular climbing venue. It has a number of summer rock routes, but it's in winter that it really comes into its own – there are dozens of climbs of all grades.

When I interviewed Sir Chris Bonington, veteran of the Eiger, Everest and a near-fatal experience on the Ogre, he told me the only time he really thought he was going to die was on Lochnagar. He was making a winter ascent with his brother in 2000. His brother fell, hauling Sir Chris off an insecure belay. Protection he'd placed lower down held, but as he fell he had time to think – I'm done for!

A great option for Munro-baggers is a complete circuit of the five White Mounth Munros – Lochnagar, Carn a' Choire Bhoidheach, Carn an t-Sagairt Mor, Cairn Bannoch and Broad Cairn.

It's not as strenuous as it sounds – in fact I don't think you'll find an "easier" five-Munro circuit. Take in Lochnagar first – once the initial ascent is out the way the rest of the day is like a high-level moorland walk. It's fantastic ground. The round is about 28km (17.4 miles) with 1300m (4265ft) of ascent and takes strong walkers about eight hours.

The route I recommend here, however, takes in Lochnagar as a single Munro.

Descent is along the Glas-Allt – a lovely stream that tumbles down the glen with a picturesque waterfall. It also includes a visit to the Glas-Allt-Shiel royal lodge, where Queen Victoria spent lots of time. One of the lodge's outbuildings is now an open bothy – a stay here is ideal for a winter ascent of the hill.

THE ROUTE

There's a pay-and-display car park at the end of the single-track road that leads up Glen Muick from Ballater.

From here, head past the small visitor centre and toilet block before leaving the woods and turning right, heading across the flat, grassy plain to the stone-built estate buildings a few hundred metres away.

The path is excellent throughout and leads past the buildings and through a small section of woodland before meeting a track that leads west.

After about 3km (1.8 miles) of fairly gentle but steady ascent, the track curves to the north. After a short distance, the clear path for Lochnagar breaks off to the left.

After a brief descent the path climbs to the bealach shared by Lochnagar and the Meikle Pap – which is worth an ascent for the magnificent views of its grand neighbour. An alternative for a good

GEORGE GORDON BYRON

The poet George Gordon Byron was born in London in 1788 and moved to Aberdeenshire with his mother, following his father's death, around 1792.

The young aristocrat remained in Scotland until he was 10. On the death of his great uncle in the same year, 1798, he inherited the title Lord Byron.

Byron's time in Scotland obviously left an impression on him. One of his most celebrated works is 'Lachin y Gair', otherwise known as 'Dark Lochnagar'. The last verse is perhaps the best known:

Years have rolled on, Lochnagar, since I left you,
 Years must elapse, ere I tread you again:
Nature of verdure and flowers has bereft you,
 Yet still are you dearer than Albion's plain:
England! thy beauties are tame and domestic,
 To one who has roved on the mountains afar:
Oh! for the crags that are wild and majestic,
 The steep, frowning glories of dark Lochnagar.

view is to continue to the lip of the corrie – Lochnagar's cliffs, and the lochan which lends its name to the hill, are impressive. A fine photo op.

The main Lochnagar path leads up a steep rocky section known as The Ladder. Snow can lie late here.

Above The Ladder, simply follow the lip of the corrie. An ascent of about 70m (230ft) leads to Cac Carn Mor. From there it's about 0.5km (0.3 miles) to the summit – a rock outcrop known as Cac Carn Beag.

Return to Cac Carn Mor from where a path south-east can be picked up. It leads directly down the Glas-Allt, past the wonderful 50m (164ft) waterfall and on to the royal lodge. From there, follow the Land Rover track along the shore of Loch Muick, turning right at the head of the loch, then left after roughly 1km (0.6 miles) and back to the visitor centre.

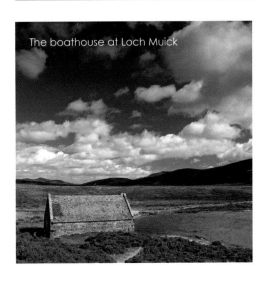

The boathouse at Loch Muick

Braeriach from Sgorr Dubh Mor

Did You Know?

At 1296m (4252ft), mighty Braeriach is the third-highest mountain in the UK.

Coire Bhrochain

50
Braeriach

THE great mountain massif we call the Cairngorms is divided into three sections by two deep passes.

The eastern Munros of Ben Avon and Beinn a' Bhuiridh are separated from the central Cairngorms by the Lairig an Laoigh.

The enormous bulk of Braeriach dominates the western portion, across the divide of the famous Lairig Ghru.

It's a huge mountain and not easily reached – even the shortest approach is a hike of more than 10km (6.2 miles). But like most things that are a wee bit more difficult, the rewards are all the sweeter.

As part of the great tundra-like environment of the Cairngorms, walking here is an experience unique in the UK. Walks-in are long, the routes – on superb paths – never hugely steep, and it feels like you're gradually leaving your regular, everyday world behind to enter a place where nature reigns supreme still.

Braeriach summit is the highest point of the western plateau, tucked in its north-east corner. West and south of the main summit, several tops rise gently from the undulating plateau, none of them under 1200m (3937ft).

On all sides, except the south, huge corries are scooped from the mountain. Traversing the rim of the eastern corries to neighbouring Munros Sgor an Lochan

Pronunciation: Bray-ree-ach
Meaning: brindled upland
Height: 1296m (4252ft); Rank: 3
OS Landranger Maps 36 & 43
Summit grid ref: NN953999 (cairn)

Uaine and Cairn Toul is a wonderful high-level outing. The airy walk – on a good day – feels like you're floating above the Lairig Ghru, the ground falling away dramatically into the deep corries beneath you.

Across Glen Dee, Ben Macdui – the only mountain in the area higher than Braeriach – and Carn a' Mhaim form a formidable wall of solid granite.

The best way to get a proper feel for the hill – for the area – is to turn your visit into a bit of an expedition. Pick a good weather window and combine the Munro with others in the area with an overnight stop at Corrour bothy – which can get very busy – or better yet, a camp on the high plateau. There's a lovely green spot just above the bothy, at the bealach between Devil's Point and Cairn Toul. It lies just above Munro height at 915m (3002ft) with freshwater springs bursting from the earth.

It's a wonderful spot, with mighty Macdui looming in the east. It's a camp you won't forget.

NEAREST TOWN: Aviemore is about 18km (11.2 miles) to the north-west. A bustling town in the heart of the Cairngorms, it has a railway station, a wide variety of accommodation, bars and restaurants, and several equipment shops – plus a couple of cracking chippies!

RECOMMENDED ROUTE
Start grid ref: NN985074
Distance: 21km (13.1 miles)
Ascent: 1250m (4101ft)
Time: 8hrs

THE ROUTE

The most direct way of climbing Braeriach is from the Sugarbowl Car Park on the road into the Cairngorm Mountain ski centre in Coire Cas. It's on Forestry Commission ground and there's a fee for all-day parking.

A superb path takes you over a bridge on Allt Mor, then runs high on the opposite bank. It takes you through the famous Chalamain Gap, the unmistakable notch that takes you to the Lairig Ghru. It's very rocky and boulder-strewn, which takes some walkers by surprise.

Once through the Gap and on to the Lairig Ghru, you cross a stream and pick up another path that takes you south-west on to Sron na Lairig. A fairly short descent south to a col is followed by a climb, south-west at first, then west, of about 150m (492ft) to the summit. It's a wonderful perch, with the great cliffs of the corries nearby. The return can be made by retracing your steps.

Braeriach can be climbed via Gleann Einich, from Whitewell. It's slightly longer but – if treated as a there-and-back – can be cycled for much of the way, before

Lairig Ghru from Sron na Lairig

SCOTLAND'S GLACIER

The sphinx snow patch is the closest thing Scotland has to a glacier – the semi-permanent patch is thought to have completely melted just seven times since the 1600s.

Found in Braeriach's Garbh Coire Mor (Big Rough Corrie), it takes its name from the climbs above it – Sphinx Gully is a winter Grade 2; Sphinx Ridge a Grade 3 (or summer V. Diff).

Records show the patch disappeared in 1933, 1953, 1959, 1996, 2003, 2006 and 2017.

Expert Iain Cameron records snow-patch survival in Scotland. His findings are published annually by the British Meteorological Society. Iain reckons the ground beneath the patch has been exposed to daylight for no more than a few months in total in the last 300 years. As a result, the granite in this area is a vibrant pink, compared to that of its surroundings, as vegetation – even moss and lichen – doesn't get time to establish itself.

Did You Know?

The Wells of Dee are pools fed by a spring that rises on Braeriach, which then form the River Dee and flow to the sea at Aberdeen. At 1220m (4003ft), it's the highest source of any major river in the UK.

Sron na Lairig from Braeriach

leaving your bike for the final third or so of the route.

It can also be climbed from Achlean, in Glen Feshie, via the excellent Foxhunter's Path – a much longer route, but one taking you through beautiful native pine forest in its lower reaches.

Ben Macdui from Braeriach

GAELIC GLOSSARY 📖

THE names of most Munros are Gaelic – or certainly derive from Gaelic – although Norse also had an influence in the far north and west. Gaelic names tend to be descriptive of a hill's character – its shape, size, position, terrain and even colour – and a little bit of knowledge of the language can be very useful for the hillwalker. For example, *sgor* – or sometimes *sgurr* – means "jagged peak". *Gaoithe* means "windy". So if you plan to climb the Cairngorm Munro of Sgor Gaoith, you'll know it might be an idea to pack that extra fleece.

Below is a brief list of Gaelic words commonly seen in hill names and their English translation. If you're unfamiliar with Gaelic then it's worth remembering that the Gaelic *bh* and *mh* are like the "v" sound in English when attempting pronunciation.

abhainn	river		**each**	horse
allt	stream		**eas**	waterfall
aonach	ridge		**eilde**	hind
ban/bhan	white		**eun**	bird
beag	little		**fionn**	white, fair
bealach	pass, col		**gabhar/gobhar**	goat
ben/beinn/bheinn	hill or mountain		**gaoithe/gaoth**	wind
bidean/bidein	pinnacle		**garbh**	rough
binnein	peak		**geal**	white
buachaille	herdsman		**ghlas/glas**	green-grey
bhuidhe/buidhe	yellow		**gorm**	blue
carn/cairn/charn	stony, stone pile		**iolaire**	eagle
clach	rock		**laogh/laoigh**	calf
ciche/cioch	breast		**leith/liath**	grey
choire/coire	corrie		**mam/mhaim**	breast
craig/creag	crag/cliff		**maol**	bald head
damh	stag		**meall**	rounded hill
dearg	red		**mheadhoin/vane**	middle
dhubh/dubh	black		**mhor/mor/more**	big

mullach	summit		**sron**	nose
ruaidh	red		**stob**	point, peak
sgor/sgurr	jagged peak		**stuc**	sharp peak
socach	snout		**tom**	hill
spidean	pinnacle		**uaine**	green

SCOTLAND'S OTHER HILLS

OF course, there's more to Scotland's hills than merely Munros.

Corbetts – hills between 2500ft and 2999ft (762m and 914m). They must have a drop of at least 500ft (152m) between any higher neighbouring hill. There are 222 Corbetts, named after John Rooke Corbett, who compiled the list in the 1920s.

Grahams – hills between 2000ft and 2499ft (610m and 762m). These are named in memory of Fiona Graham. There are 220 Grahams. They must have a prominence of 150m (490ft), reflecting the fact the list was compiled in the metric era.

Donalds – there are 89 Donalds, named for Percy Donald who compiled his list in 1935. These are hills found in the Scottish Lowlands, and must have a minimum height of 2000ft (610m).

THE MUNROS
A PHOTOGRAPHER'S VIEW

by Keith Fergus

LIKE many photographers, my love of capturing images began with my love of hillwalking. Heading into the mountains, invariably one of our 282 Munros, I felt compelled to take photographs of the people I was with and the mountains I climbed. But, most of all, it was to record the extraordinary scenery that Scotland's mountains offer – even when, on a number of occasions, the view from the summit was a cairn shrouded in mist.

Initially the photographs were there to provide tangible memories of days in the hills with not much thought given to composition, light or even equipment; a cheap Vivitar 35mm camera with an even cheaper lens was my first camera. However, as time went on, I became aware of photographers such as Colin Prior, Colin Baxter and Gordon Stainforth, who took mountain photography to another level. I began to study their images to work out why they resonated with me so much.

One reason was the time at which their photographs were taken. And so I began to head out into the mountains early in the morning and late in the day – sometimes camping out – in the hope that I could capture the gorgeous light found at these times. My trips began to take more planning and I studied maps to pick out the best vantage points. I thought, too, more about composition, invested in some better equipment and bought a tripod, perhaps the most vital component of a mountain photographer's kit bag.

Yet, most importantly of all, I began to really think about the final photograph, and how to take more time over an image. Slowly, my photography improved, primarily by taking fewer photographs as my focus became about quality over quantity. Over time I have built up a strong portfolio of Scotland's Munros, along with some incredible memories.

I've listed below a few things that help me with my mountain photography. It isn't an exhaustive list and can easily be adjusted to suit your own needs, but it's one that works for me. But the most important thing you can do is simply get out into the mountains and get snapping.

EQUIPMENT

The equipment I use for my photographs never supersedes anything that will keep me safe on the mountains; waterproofs, spare clothes, hat, gloves, food, water, map and compass should be a priority. Be prepared for your rucksack to weigh a bit more in your pursuit of mountain images, and for some hanging about waiting for the right light. So keep warm.

Images can now be taken on different devices (phones, tablets, compact cameras), and shared on a variety of social media outlets. Yet something I hear regularly is that the final image never lives up to expectations. Many think the more expensive the camera the better the final image will be. Actually, the type of camera is almost irrelevant – it is what you do with it that's significant. Having said that, all of my images are taken with a Canon DSLR (Digital Single Reflex) camera, but some of the topics covered below are applicable to whatever device you use.

As well as the camera body, a decent wide-angle and telephoto lens will cover most photographic opportunities while a good sturdy tripod is a worthwhile investment. This slows the whole photographic process down. Furthermore, in low light, exposures of more than one second will be the norm. If you mount your camera on a tripod, your photographs will be crisp and, if focused correctly, sharp.

A simple hot-shoe spirit level can be mounted on the camera, making it easy to keep your horizon straight. In most landscape photography situations a neutral density graduated filter will be necessary to balance the contrast within a scene – typically between the bright sky and considerably darker land. This optical filter (usually glass or plastic) attaches to the front of your lens with the dark part of the filter covering the bright areas of the scene. By then setting the correct exposure, detail can be held across the whole image. A polariser filter is also very useful. Again, attached to the lens, a polariser absorbs reflected light and consequently intensifies colours.

Spare batteries and camera memory cards are always a good idea, and a head torch is essential if you are out walking around sunrise/sunset – you need to be able to see what you're doing.

COMPOSITION

Perhaps the most important aspect of photography is composition. My best tip is "keep it simple" – what is left out of the image is often more important than what is kept in. The rule of thirds is often deemed the ideal compositional technique – this sees the image split into nine equal squares. But I tend to focus on what will hold the viewer's attention. This may be a cloud-studded sky or a nearby mountain peak. A path, ridge or wall will help grab the viewer and draw their eye through the image. And don't forget about introducing people into your images, which can add scale and perspective.

TIME OF DAY

The golden hours (the hour after sunrise and the hour before sunset) are generally regarded as the best time to shoot landscapes as the intense warm colours of the rising/setting sun and the long raking shadows can help lift an image from good to great. Even so, great images can be taken at any time of the day. So it's important to go out with your camera whenever you can – inclement conditions can produce some of the most dramatic imagery.

PLANNING

When I have chosen a particular mountain to photograph I will use a number of online resources – such as the Mountain Weather Information Service (www.mwis.org.uk) and the Met Office (www.metoffice.gov.uk) to check weather conditions before venturing out. I'll also use an Ordnance Survey or Harveys Map, not only to work out my route, but to judge what may be the best vantage points for photography. (Bear in mind rule number one – the summit doesn't always offer the best view). A sunset/sunrise compass helps me ascertain the position of the sun at different times of the day throughout the year – similarly the Photographer's Ephemeris (www.photoephemeris.com) is a remarkable online resource.

But remember – there is really no substitute for being out exploring the mountains and looking for your own favourite views.

Outdoor writer and photographer Keith Fergus is the author of 15 books, including Great Scottish Journeys *(2017). He also publishes the Scottish Horizons range of calendars and greeting cards.*

Keith Fergus on Ben Lomond

SOURCES

Allan, Geoff, *The Scottish Bothy Bible* (Wild Things Publishing, 2017)

Anderson, Rab and Prentice, Tom, *The Grahams and the Donalds, SMC Hillwalkers' Guide* (Scottish Mountaineering Trust, 2015)

Bailey, Dan, *Great Mountain Days in Scotland: 50 Classic Hillwalking Challenges* (Cicerone, 2012)

Barton, Bob and Wright, Blyth, *A Chance in a Million? Scottish Avalanches* (Scottish Mountaineering Trust, 2nd edition, 2000)

Bearhop, Derek A., *Munro's Tables and Other Tables of Lower Hills* (Scottish Mountaineering Trust, revised and edited, 1997)

Bennet, Donald and Anderson, Rab (eds), *The Munros, SMC Hillwalkers' Guide* (Scottish Mountaineering Trust, revised 2013)

Brown, Hamish, *Hamish's Mountain Walk* (Sandstone Press, 2010. First published 1978)

Butterfield, Irvine, *The High Mountains of Britain and Ireland* (Diadem Books, 1986)

Crofton, Ian, *A Dictionary of Scottish Phrase and Fable* (Birlinn, 2012)

Dempster, Andrew, *Classic Mountain Scrambles in Scotland* (Luath, new edition, 2016)

Drummond, Peter, *Scottish Hill Names: Their Origin and Meaning* (Scottish Mountaineering Trust, 2007)

Johnstone, Scott; Brown, Hamish, and Bennet, Donald (eds) *The Corbetts and Other Scottish Hills, SMC Hillwalkers' Guide* (Scottish Mountaineering Trust, 1990)

Kew, Steve, *Walking the Munros. Volume 1: Southern, Central and Western Highlands* (Cicerone, 3rd edition, 2017)

Kew, Steve, *Walking the Munros. Volume 2: Northern Highlands and the Cairngorms* (Cicerone, 2nd edition, 2017)

Langmuir, Eric, *Mountaincraft and Leadership* (Mountain Training Boards of England and Scotland, 4th edition, 2013)

Mackay, George, *Scottish Place Names* (Waverley, 2nd edition, 2011)

Mackenzie, Alexander, *The Prophecies of the Brahan Seer* (Lang Syne, 1989. First published 1877)

Marsh, Terry, *The Isle of Skye* (Cicerone, 3rd edition, 2009)

McNeish, Cameron, *The Munros* (Lomond Books, 1996)

McNeish, Cameron, *There's Always The Hills* (Sandstone Press, 2018)

Mitchell, Ian R., *Scotland's Mountains Before the Mountaineers* (Luath, 2013)

Murray, W. H., *Mountaineering in Scotland & Undiscovered Scotland* (Baton Wicks, new edition, 1997)

Swire, Otta, *Skye: The Island and its Legends* (Birlinn, 2016. First published 1952)

The Scottish Rights of Way and Access Society, *Scottish Hill Tracks* (Scottish Mountaineering Trust, 5th edition, 2011)

Townsend, Chris, *World Mountain Ranges: Scotland* (Cicerone, 2010)

WEBSITES

www.hill-bagging.co.uk

www.munromagic.com

www.nhs.co.uk

www.outdooraccess-scotland.scot

www.smc.org.uk

www.walkhighlands.co.uk

ACKNOWLEDGEMENTS

Thank you to everyone who has shared great hill days and mountain adventures with me over the years. In particular:

Alex MacLennan
Ron Dorn
Andy Buchan
Andy Hood
Stephen Flynn
Eunice Coop
John Berry
Donald Irvine
Dave Kingswood

Phil Barlow
Noelle Ryan
Malcolm Hodgins
Kevin Murray
Fraser Gold
Stuart Wallis
Barbara Carnegie
Jon Moss
Billy McIsaac

Drew Crawford
Iain Wilson
Derek Hall
Allan Carr
Stephen Meldrum
Alan Gilliland
Ian Gilmour
Shirley & Jim
 Mackenzie

Nick Harrington
Andy Baker
Fi Russell & Wispa,
and all at the MMC

Special thanks to
Cameron McNeish
for his inspiration
and advice.

Glen Affric